PLACES IN

JORDAN

A Pocket Grand Tour

FRANCIS RUSSELL

F

FRANCES LINCOLN LIMITED
PUBLISHERS

CONTENTS

For my godmother Cynthia Wood,
who half a century ago indulged
my taste for systematic sightseeing
with such spirit; and for my
godchildren, Georgiana Campbell,
Poppy Macdonald-Buchanan, Amelia
de Rougemont, Victoria Brudenell,
Ralph Dundas, Victoria Sassoon
and Alexander Grant.

Frances Lincoln Limited
4 Torriano Mews
Torriano Avenue
London NW5 2RZ
www.franceslincoln.com

Places in Jordan
Copyright © Frances Lincoln Limited 2012
Text and photographs copyright ©
Francis Russell 2012
First Frances Lincoln edition 2012

A catalogue record for this book is available
from the British Library.

ISBN: 978-0-7112-3269-3

Printed and bound in China
1 2 3 4 5 6 7 8 9

Page 2 **Umm ar-Rasas: Church of St Stephen, mosaic of Mefa.** Below **Qualaat ar-Rabadh from the south-east.**

INTRODUCTION

'Welcome to Jordan': the message is on every schoolboy's tongue. It is for the tourist to discover what this means in a country carved out of a disintegrated empire in the twentieth century, a land the relative poverty of which in natural resources is for the sightseer most abundantly balanced by the survival of so much spectacular evidence of the past.

It is with due humility that I endeavour to do justice to this evidence. My old friend Brinsley Ford, when told that he was an art historian, indignantly if not wholly correctly denied this, adding: 'I am a damned aesthete!' I myself am neither an archaeologist nor a historian: I am merely a sightseer. Such specialized knowledge as I may have lies in other spheres. But I like to think I am a tolerably efficient tourist. For me mere foundations have a limited appeal, unless these happen to be in places of great natural beauty. I have a preference for unexcavated sites, or at least for those where reconstruction has been restrained. I like to linger, and to observe the fall and movement of light. And I am deeply impressed by the way the Jordanian authorities have protected a remarkable patrimony and understand the value of the great monuments in their care in our fast-changing world.

The kingdom of Jordan takes its name from the great river that flows from the mountains of Syria and the Lebanon to the north and drains southwards to the Dead Sea. The frontiers of the kingdom are bounded on the west by the Rift Valley, and thus by the river itself from near the southern tip of the Lake of Galilee, by the Dead Sea and the Wadi Araba southwards to the head of the Gulf of Aqaba, on the north by the

Petra: view from the top of the Deir.

river Yarmuk and beyond this and to the east and south by the more arbitrary lines across the Hauran and the deserts laid down at Versailles after the First World War that reach the coast of the Red Sea just south of Aqaba.

The territory of Trans-Jordan, as this eastern section of the land that had formed part of Syria and which was mandated to England was initially known, had seen many former rulers: the unidentified Neolithic people who settled at Jawa; the ancient kingdoms of Ammon, Moab and Edom documented in the Old Testament, and that of the Jews, whose city of Jerusalem can be seen from King Herod's castle of Machaerus; the Nabataeans of Petra, Arabs from the south, who like the Jews submitted to Rome, by whom Syria was annexed in 64 BC; the Romans, whose desert forts long protected the urban civilization represented so splendidly at Jerash; their Byzantine successors, whose mosaics at Madaba and elsewhere still testify to a brilliant theocratic empire that held Syria until the decisive Arab victory at the Yarmuk in 636; the Umayyads of Damascus, builders of the remarkable desert palaces; their Abbasid nemeses from Humayma, who ruled Syria and much of the then civilized world from Baghdad; the Crusaders, who controlled their Oultrejourdaine from Montreal (Shobak) and Karak, and were in their turn ejected from this, although not from Jerusalem, by Saladin, a cousin of whom had previously built the castle of Ajlun; the Mamelukes, whose power was based in Cairo and for a time chose Karak as their administrative centre, who finally drove the Crusaders from the Holy Land; and, from 1516 until they were driven from Palestine and Syria in 1917–18, the Ottomans, who ruled from Constantinople, and to whom the area was of importance not least because it was crossed by the route of the Haj, the pilgrimage to Mecca.

The Hashemites, descendants of Mohammed's daughter, Fatima, who had controlled the Holy Places of Islam as Grand Sharifs or Amirs of Mecca, became allies of the English during the First World War.

They seemed natural successors to the territories in Syria that the Ottomans has forfeited. But their prospects were clouded by the conflicting undertakings made by Britain and her allies in pursuit of victory. Feisal was driven from Damascus by the French, to be awarded the unstable entity of Iraq, made up of parts of two Ottoman governates, by the British, the eastern section of whose mandate in the former Syria, comprising the territory of the modern kingdom, became as it were the client emirate of his brother, Abdullah, controlled from Jerusalem by the High Commissioner. As in Syria, where the French restored numerous monuments in an exemplary manner, and Iraq, where under Gertrude Bell archaeology was seen as a way of fostering a sense of nationhood, the mandatory authorities were keenly aware of the importance of protecting the monuments in their care. Successive high commissioners for Palestine and Trans-Jordan tried to balance the ultimately incompatible claims of the indigenous inhabitants of Palestine and the Zionist settlers; but in the aftermath of the Second World War the British position ceased to be tenable. Transjordan (shorn of its hyphen) became an independent kingdom, under Abdullah, on 25 May 1946. The British withdrawal from Palestine some two years later led to a war between the Palestinians and the Israelis, in which, despite contacts between the king and Israeli politicians, Transjordan proved to be the only effective ally of the former. At the end of the war the kingdom was in control of much of the West Bank and of part of Jerusalem, taking on in addition responsibility for half a million of the refugees who had been displaced by the new state of Israel. In recognition of these developments, King Abdullah renamed his country Jordan in 1950. He was to be assassinated a year later.

When Jordan became independent in 1946, King Abdullah retained a number of the Englishmen who had worked under the Mandate. The best known of these was, of course, General Sir John Glubb, Glubb Pasha, whose Arab Legion fought as conspicuously in the struggle of 1948–9 as it had in the Second World War. Equally remarkable in his very different field was G. Lankester Harding, Chief Curator of Jordanian Antiquities from 1936 and subsequently Director, whose *The Antiquities of Jordan* (London, 1959) remains after half a century the best and most elegantly expressed general survey of the subject, despite the great archaeological advances of the intervening years; he certainly deserved the honour of being buried at Jerash, about which he had written so fluently. Harding and his Jordanian successors, who consistently enjoyed the support of King Abdullah and of his remarkable grandson, King Hussein, who reigned from 1953 until 1999, have presided over a long and continuing programme of both excavation and restoration: and there can be few countries where the evidence of the past has been, and continues to be, treated with such consistent respect.

In many ways Harding and his counterparts were fortunate. Elsewhere archaeological sites had been raided by the enterprising since the Renaissance, not least in the nineteenth century. The remoteness of the land beyond the Jordan and the Ottoman inability to control the tribes that dominated the area discouraged both travellers and souvenir hunters. Palmyra and Baalbek had been known to members of the European merchant community at Aleppo, long before these were studied by Wood and Dawkins in 1751. But it was not until 1812 that John Lewis Burckhardt reached Petra, and then only briefly; he was followed in 1818 by Irby and Mangles, who had had their names carved on so many of the monuments of Egypt and did so in the Treasury, by Comte Leon de Laborde in 1828, by the American J. L. Stephens in 1836 and the bibliophile and historian of Christian art Lord Lindsay a year later, by the American Edward Robinson in 1838 and by the painter David Roberts in 1839.

But the Bedouin remained wary of travellers, and as late as 1840 Austen Henry Layard and his companions were attacked by local tribesmen in the ruins. Many travellers of the ensuing period were clergymen drawn to sought to identify places mentioned in the Bible at the very time that the authority of this seemed to some to be challenged by the work of Charles Darwin: Dean Stanley, who later escorted the Prince of Wales to the Holy Land and was instrumental in the foundation of the Palestine Exploration Fund, in 1865; Canon Tristram, author of *The Land of Moab* (London, 1873), who explored an area that had only recently been pacified; and the Revd W. M. Thompson, whose *The Land and the Book* went through numerous editions, among others. Much territory was accurately surveyed and photographs were taken, most notably by Sarjent Henry Phillips, RE (1867), Tancrede Dumas (1875) and C. A. Hornstein (1895). The magic of the places they and others recorded is expressed with an unequalled eloquence by Gertrude Bell in *The Desert and the Sown* (London, 1903) and in her letters.

Bell and other writers including T. E. Lawrence (*The Seven Pillars of Wisdom*) did justice to the extraordinary beauty of the landscapes of Jordan. So many of these live in the memory: the verdant prosperity of the valleys that gave life to the towns of the Decapolis; the basalt wilderness to the east; the sun-drenched wadis on the approach to Qasr al-Tuba, patrolled still by expectant birds; the plunging views over the Dead Sea from Machaerus and Mount Nebo; the drama of the descent to and climb up from the Wadi Hasa, with the dark silhouette of Khirbet Tannur, the extraordinary contrasts of Petra, where the narrow siq opens to a wide valley flanked by cliffs, and high up, beyond the Deir, a natural break though a low wall of rock leads to a small high place that is literally suspended above gorges that fall away to the Wadi Araba; the Wadi Rum, which Lawrence made his own, with towering cliffs above the level golden sand, and evidence everywhere of the passage of early peoples; and the eyrie, menacing beauty of the Wadi Feinan, among the oldest of untrammelled post-industrial landscapes, where Rome despatched her Christian prisoners to process copper with the ruthless efficiency that so long sustained her power.

Because so many of the major sites of Jordan have been spared intrusive development it is still possible for the visitor to see these though the eyes of early travellers, and anyone planning a tour should try to study R. S. Abujaber and F. Cobbing's *Beyond the River: Ottoman Transjordan in Original Photographs* (London, 2005). The archaeological literature is vast. For the amateur, armed with his copy of Lankester Harding, the following publications, listed in chronological order of subject, are of particular use: D. Kennedy and R. Bewley, *Ancient Jordan from the Air* (London, 2004); S. W. Helms, *Jawa: Lost City of the Black Desert* (London, 1981); J. Turner, *Petra and the Lost Kingdom of the Nabataeans* (London, 2001); I. Browning, *Petra* (London, 1989); K. Butcher, *Roman Syria and the Near East* (London, 2003); D. Kennedy and D. Riley, *Rome's Desert Frontier from the Air* (London, 1990); I. Browning, *Jerash and the Decapolis* (London, 1982); Museum with No Frontiers Exhibition, *The Umayyads: The Rise of Islamic Art* (Amman and Vienna, 2000); and W. Muller-Wiener, *Castles of the Crusaders* (New York and Toronto, 1966). For a kaleidoscopic view try *Studies in the History and Archaeology of Jordan*, edited by A. Hadidi (three volumes, Amman, 1982). No English writer of today has done more to record the artistic legacy of Jordan in successive publications than Jane Taylor, whose generosity with advice I gratefully acknowledge.

The independent tourist will need at least one guidebook for help with practical matters. While the comprehensively well-informed *Blue Guide* (S. Rollin and J. Streetly, London and New York, 1996) is in a class of its own, Ivan Mannheim's *Footprint Jordan Handbook* (Bath, 2000) and Matthew Teller's *Rough Guide* (London, 2009) are more helpful for practical information.

The Anglo-Saxon may find Jordan uncomfortably warm for determined sightseeing in the summer. My first visit was in February. It snowed as Simon Barnes and I drove down the King's Highway, and he very understandably remained in the car while I paced the whitened walls of the legionary fortress at 'Udruh. We settled in the nearest hotel to the approach to Petra, and I set out alone in swirling mist. Two riders passed me as I walked through the siq, which was already echoing with the sound of water tumbling from the rock; I made towards the temple and at length saw a fire, round which a cheerful group of Bedu salesmen were gathered. They took me in. And it was in their tent that I abandoned surplus clothes and cameras in the days that followed, when a fierce sunlight brought out the colours of the rock and too quickly melted the snow on the crests of the jebel. But, bright as this was, the sun could not dispel the winter and I have never been as cold as when, a few days later, I was caught on the exposed heights of the Crusader fortress of Al-Wu'eira by horizontal hail that cut into every pore. More often I have been to Jordan at Christmas, when the beauty of the low light reconciles me to the shortness of the days. In an ideal world one would, of course, wait to be told that rain had fallen, and arrange to travel a fortnight later to witness the flowering of the desert, but most of us, alas, need to plan at longer notice.

I am indebted to Simon Barnes for his forbearance on our visit to Jordan in 1990, to the many Jordanians who have made me feel so welcome in their country, to Nickolas Neibauer and his colleagues for help and hospitality at Feinan, and to Mark Allen and John Hemming for their advice. Once again Emile Joachim at Richard Caplan has been unfailingly helpful with photographic advice. Miriam Winslow-Alio has helped me to control my word processor. I am most grateful to John Nicoll for agreeing to publish this book and to the patience and understanding of his colleagues at Frances Lincoln, particularly Anne Askwith, Andrew Dunn and Emma O'Bryen.

1. AMMAN

Most visitors to Jordan fly to and leave from Amman. This was chosen as his capital by the Emir Abdullah in 1921, and bears a historic name. Early travellers came to see the substantial remains of Roman Philadelphia and saw rather more than we can today, for the place had been more or less abandoned for a millennium, and the ruins spared the attrition of urban development. Modern Amman has grown exponentially. The process begun by the Emir was accentuated by the influx of refugees from Palestine, both in 1949 and in 1967; and a wave of recent development was stimulated in part by the more recent arrival of entrepreneurs from Iraq. Amman has become a dynamic city. But for the sightseer, confused by the way this now sprawls across the valley of the Zarqa and its tributaries, stretching westwards into the Balqa hills, Amman does not stand comparison with the great historic cities of the Near East, Damascus or Aleppo or Beirut. With the exception of the brave new Jordan Museum, it is indeed for dead rather than living monuments that Amman now deserves to be visited.

The area now subsumed within the conurbation has been occupied, at least intermittently, since very early times. Thus at 'Ain Ghazel there was a substantial Neolithic settlement, now best known for the strange pottery figures that constitute perhaps the earliest extant corpus of sculpture in the Near East. The site of the citadel on the Jabal al-Qal'a was fortified in about 1800 BC, during the Bronze Age. Some six hundred years later the Ammonites arrived, choosing it as their capital, or 'great city', Rabbath Ammon. Over two hundred years later King David took Ammon. But his successors eventually had to yield to a new superpower, Assyria, which in turn was succeeded by Babylon, under King Nebuchadnezzar II, and by Persia, under Cyrus. In 332 BC Nebuchadnezzar's descendant Darius was defeated by Alexander, after whose death the region was fought over by two of his successors, Ptolemy of Egypt and Seleucus, who reigned over much of Asia Minor and Syria from Antioch. Ptolemy II Philadelphus recovered it from the Seleucids and renamed it Ammon Philadelphia. The Seleucids under Antiochus III regained control in 198 BC, but subsequently there seems to have been a Nabataean presence. Pompey secured the whole region for Rome in 63 BC. As the southernmost city of the Decapolis, Philadelphia became part of Pompey's province of Syria. But when the Nabataean kingdom was absorbed under Trajan in AD 106, the city was transferred to the new province of Arabia. It was evidently a place of some importance under the Byzantines and, after the Arab conquest in 635, was maintained by the Umayyads as the regional capital, now in deference to its past renamed Amman. Decline set in with the Abbasids, who ruled from Baghdad rather than Damascus and despite their former association with Humayma had little interest in the area. Early photographs show the ruins in picturesque isolation. Things began to change in 1878, when displaced Circassians were resettled at Amman as part of an Ottoman strategy to control the Bedouin tribes.

The obvious place to start a circuit of the monuments of the city is the citadel crowning the Jebel al-Qal'a, a roughly L-shaped hill that lent itself naturally to defence. A modern road climbs to the lower eastern terrace of this that retains part of its early wall. Paths from the visitor centre lead to the upper terraces. Keep to the left to see what remains of the original gate, which was reached by a steep road up from the lower town, and look across to the justly celebrated theatre cut into the opposite side of the valley. Further west there is a good stretch of the wall, with a fine Abbasid tower built of bossed blocks. The material for this was partly pillaged from the hexastyle Corinthian Temple of Hercules set on a podium within a temenos immediately to the north. Two columns of the portico have been reinstated, while the drums of others lie tumbled where they fell. An inscription establishes that Geminius Marcianus,

governor of the Province of Arabia in 162–6, dedicated the temple to the co-Emperors Marcus Aurelius and Lucius Verus.

From the temple my inclination would be to head past the former museum for the west section of the town wall, which hangs above a narrower valley, and follow this northwards to the west gate, before crossing to the centre of the hill, where a massive irregular court divided the large mosque, the footings of which have been restored, from the spectacular entrance to the Umayyad palace, a monumental vestibule flanked by side rooms that opens to an audience chamber or reception hall, the cruciform plan of which may represent that of an earlier church. This remarkable building is probably of the time of the Caliph Hisham (724–43). Remarkably, much of its elaborate decoration survives. Sasanian influence has been recognized, not least in the tiered decorative scheme in three registers below a cornice, with niches and blind arches resting on twin pilasters, framing panels carved with patterns of plant and other forms, including palmettes, vines, trefoils and quatrefoils. The hall seems originally to have been an open courtyard, but was subsequently roofed in wood. Comparison with early photographs shows how much the decoration has suffered in the last century. The modern roof is thus a necessary protection. There is, however, no clear authority for the dome, which does admittedly complement the semi-domes of the lateral sections of the chamber.

A door opens to a square court, on the other side of which a section of a once-colonnaded Roman road runs to a gate in the former temenos wall of what was in all probability the larger of the temples of Roman Philadelphia, distinguished by excellent masonry and a regular line of niches. The road and temenos wall apart, the area was extensively redeveloped by the Umayyads. On either side of the court there is a bayt, or group of rooms ranged round a central court. There are two

Inscription by the Temple of Hercules.

more bayts on each side of the road, those to the west responsibly left for the archaeologists of the future, and three more behind these and that to the left of the court. Here, it is thought, were the administrative quarters. The gate though the temenos wall leads to the corner of a further court, originally colonnaded on three sides, but with a substantial iwan on the north that opens to an ingeniously planned cruciform throne room, in which the ruler would, as custom dictated, have been concealed behind a curtain from those to whom audiences were accorded. Flanked by a number of substantial rooms, this inner residential section of the palace was complemented by four further bayts.

On leaving the Umayyad Palace through the great vestibule, cut to the left to see the splendid circular cistern of about 730, originally plastered, which contained 1,359 cubic metres/48,000 cubic feet of rainwater: a flight of thirty-five steps gave access to this. On the way back to the visitor centre you will pass the remains of a Byzantine church.

Although this is not encouraged, it is possible to leave the citadel by walking down between the houses below the Abbasid tower, descending a sequence of flights of steps to arrive in what was once the centre of Philadelphia and is now the heart of the commercial quarter of modern Amman. As at Pergamon and Nysa in Asia Minor, the Romans covered the river with a tunnel, so that they could build above it. Their forum, part of the colonnade of which survives, stretched to the south. This is now entered from the west, down steps to the southern colonnade. Behind it is the great theatre, which was completed in 169–77, during the reign of Marcus Aurelius. This faces north and could accommodate some 6,000 spectators, in tiers respectively of fourteen, twelve and sixteen rows. An unusual feature is a small shrine high at the top of the auditorium that is built into the hillside. Rooms to the east of the partly reconstructed stage building serve as a museum, with exhibits including fragments of Byzantine mosaics from churches at Jerash and elsewhere. Adjacent to the theatre and flanking the forum on the east is the very restored odeon.

Sarcophagus by the Museum.

The decumanus of Philadelphia ran along the wadi floor, close to the line of the modern partly arcaded Saqf Sayl Street. West of the forum, near the junction of this with the cardo maximus, which ran up the valley west of the Jabel al-Qal'a, is the last of the major buildings of Roman Philadelphia: the exceptionally large nymphaeum, the spectacular bossed-back façade of which faces Saqf Sayl Street. Two of the original three exedras to the north are in place, although the basin in front of the larger of these is an Islamic introduction. The polychrome marbles with which the structure was faced have gone, but enough decorated blocks remain for one to have at least a sense of the richness of the original decoration.

Further to the west, where the Saqf Sayl ends at Ras al-Ain ('source of the spring'), is the emphatic new building that houses the Jordan Museum. This was not open in December 2010, but will house the archaeological collection formerly displayed in the museum on the citadel. Ideally the museum should be seen before embarking on a tour of the country. There are many notable things: the remarkable plaster figures, one with striped trousers, from 'Ain Ghazel (8000–6000 BC); the exceptional Chalcolithic mural with highly stylized attendants painted in red from Teleilat Ghassul (4500–3300 BC); the Moabite stela of a ruler from Balu' (twelfth century BC); Bronze Age ivories from Pella, remounted in a cedar box; the relief of Atargatis from the Nabataean temple at Khirbet Tannur; the three copper scrolls from Qumran; the unusually fine mid-second century Roman copy of a Hellenistic statue of Icarus, his hair flying in the wind, which was found in Amman; the excellent portrait of Marcus Aurelius from the Qasr al-Bint at Petra; and the intricately carved lintel from Qasr al-Tuba, which heightens one's sense of loss at what has been taken from that much-abused Omayyad building.

2. IRAQ AL-AMIR

There is no stranger building of the Hellenistic period in the Near East than the palace at Iraq al-Amir, in the beautiful Wadi as-Sir, some 17 kilometres/10½ miles west of Amman, just beyond the eroded cliffs, cut with caves, partly artificial, from which the place takes its name, meaning 'caves of the prince'. The site was occupied in the Bronze Age, but subsequently abandoned. The palace, known now as the Qasr al-Abid ('the castle of the slave'), is thought to have been built in 182–175 BC by Hyrcanus, a descendant of Tobiah, a Jew who became Governor of Ammon in the sixth century and founded a powerful dynasty: Tobiah's name, or that of an eponymous descendant, is inscribed on two of the openings to the caves. Hyrcanus, son of Joseph and grandson of a daughter of the Sanhedrin, was sent early in his life to Egypt, for his family had been allied to the Ptolomies. His brothers, who controlled Jerusalem, were drawn into the rival Seleucid sphere, and this may explain why Hyrcanus was banished to, or withdrew beyond, the Jordan, where he engaged in perpetual warfare with the Arabs. The palace, which he is stated by the historian Josephus to have built, was apparently left unfinished on Hyrcanus' suicide in 175 BC. It is a remarkable statement of personal ambition: originally set in an artificial lake, it was the focal point of a complex of more modest buildings that hung above the lower ground to the south.

With its outsize limestone blocks, the palace must have astonished contemporaries. Josephus, writing in AD 93, was an accurate observer, recording that Hyrcanus 'built a strong fortress which was constructed entirely of white stone to the very roof and had beasts of a prodigious magnitude carved upon it. He also drew round it a great and deep moat of water' (*Antiquities of the Jews*, XII, 4, 11). The visitor will not be disappointed. I quickly succumbed in 1997: 'The valley promises little: much traffic on a narrow twisting road; and too much new building. But after however many bends the building comes into sight – & what a place – cyclopean blocks on a podium in the middle of the valley – low cliffs above, olives and figs trees, tillage, vegetables and rows of onions.' The rectangular structure, set on a larger podium, responds to the bright sunlight, the stone now a pale gold after exposure for two millennia.

Hyrcanus' palace has not survived unscathed. Because the great blocks, some of which are 6 metres/20 feet long and 3 metres/10 feet high, are only 45 centimetres/18 inches thick, the structure was vulnerable to earthquakes, and Byzantine occupants swept away evidence of the original internal arrangements. Early photographs show what had survived: two courses of cyclopean masonry, surmounted by a simple frieze, below the row of large blocks with the celebrated reliefs of lions and lionesses, which originally were surmounted by eagles, part of one of which lies

Iraq al-Amir. Above: relief of lioness. Right: the south portico.

near by. The best-preserved lions are on the west corner. More unusual is the relief of a lioness on the west wall. Equally accomplished are the two of leopards in a conglomerate stone, flushed with pink, on the lateral walls: these served as fountains. The entrance is on the north, opening to a vestibule: there are three windows in the southern counterpart to this. A staircase at the north-east corner led to the upper storey. There is now a small site museum which documents the exemplary French restoration completed in 1980.

For those with time, the caves have a strange fascination. These are cut into the cliff, two strata of which were relatively easily worked. Steps lead up from the road to the main groups. On the lower level are the two great barrel-vaulted cuttings, on the façades of which Tobiad's name is inscribed in Hebrew: a row of post holes for a timber roof shows how much detritus has accumulated in that to the east. Most of the caves are at the higher level: two have lateral extensions on the right; another, larger and partly natural, has rows of mangers cut into the walls. Further west a rock with rows of square recesses stands out from the cliff.

3. SALT

Salt is, for Jordan, a unique survival, a town that preserves the fabric of the Ottoman past. Set in the rolling Balqa hills and famed in medieval times for its gardens, Salt came to prominence under the Mamelukes, who built a major fortress there; and as a regional capital under the Ottomans it was the only town of any significance east of the Jordan. It was from Salt that early explorers of the hinterland and its antiquities set out; and in the second half of the nineteenth century the place became very prosperous. Merchants migrated from Palestine in pursuit of commercial opportunities and although Circassian refugees from Russia were resettled in the town in the 1880s, roughly half the population was Christian. Salt continued to flourish in the last years of Ottoman rule; and in 1921 it was here that Abdullah was proclaimed Emir of Trans-Jordan. The subsequent decision to transfer his capital to Amman meant that Salt became a backwater, and this, as much as the excellence of the golden local stone, ensured the survival of so much of its Ottoman fabric.

The town developed on the slopes below and opposite a hill, Al'Qala, the Mameluke fortress on which was demolished in 1840. At the southern foot of this is the Al-Ain Plaza (!), an open triangle, fronted on the south by the Abu Jaber House, now the Historic Old Salt Museum, by far the most ambitious late nineteenth-century mansion in Salt, and indeed in Jordan, the extensive front of which well expresses the eclecticism of the Ottoman *belle époque*. The museum is worth seeing as much for the warren of rooms on three floors as for the exhibits, which are well set out.

At the museum leaflets with excellent itineraries are available. Above and to the west of the building are the Khatib and Sakit houses, begun respectively in 1860 and 1879, steps between which lead up to the Said Al-Bahra Street, with, on the left, the Khlaifat House (1879–84), which like the Abu Jaber House was visited by the Emir Abdullah.

Across the plaza from the Abu Jaber House is the Daoud House of 1881, with shops on the ground floor. Above this is the former English Hospital, with the letters EH on the metal gate. An English post was established here in 1849, and the Church of the Good Shepherd was begun in 1867; the medical mission set up in 1889 became the English Hospital twenty years later. There are numerous late nineteenth-century houses on the hill, many with classicizing details and one, the Nabulsi House, with a kishet, or external projection on the upper floor. Below, on the narrow Hammam Street that runs eastwards, now lined with stalls, is the Mihayar House, with a gothic door.

At the end of Hammam Street turn right. A little way down on the left is the Tuqan House, of between 1900 and 1915, in a consciously historical style. This was built for 'Ala al-Din Tuqan (1872–1944), who in 1929 became a member of the Legislative Council and was in charge of the Department of Antiquities. The house is thus a very suitable setting for the Salt Archaeological Museum, with material, predominantly pottery, from numerous sites in the Balqa. Perhaps the most appealing exhibits are a tiny bone dog of 1500–1200 BC from Katerit as-Samra and two shards with writing in Aramaic of 500–300 BC from Tell Nimrin.

Façade of the Abu Jaber House.

4. JERASH

Nowhere perhaps is the sightseer granted a fuller experience of the *douceur de vivre* of urban life in Roman Syria than at Jerash, the classical Gerasa, set in a generous valley among the still fertile hills of Gilead. Founded under Alexander the Great's Seleucid successors, Gerasa was one of the ten cities of the Decapolis, stretching from Philadelphia to Qanawat in the Jebel al-Arab (now in Syria), which by the first century BC were subject to the Hasmonaeans of Judaea. A period of instability was resolved by Pompey's campaign of 64 BC, and Gerasa was absorbed in the Roman province of Syria. Peace brought prosperity, which was only briefly interrupted by the Jewish Revolt of AD 63. The Hellenistic city was greatly expanded, and its walled successor was largely laid out on either side of the river Chrysorhoas in the first century AD, with a colonnaded cardo maximus crossed by two other principal streets and a series of public buildings. A road linked the city with the Via Nova Traiana from Bosra to the Red Sea, which like the railways of nineteenth-century Prussia had a dual commercial and military function. Hadrian's visit in 129–30 emphasized the importance of Gerasa, and was commemorated by a splendid arch, so it comes as something of a surprise to realize that at its zenith the city may have had a population of no more than 25,000.

The third century was not kind to Roman Syria, but the rise of Christianity was matched by renewed prosperity, and of the fifteen churches of the city that of Bishop Genesius is of 611, on the eve of Chosroes II's invasion of Syria. After Syria fell to the Arabs in 636, Gerasa evidently became a backwater, and earthquakes in the eighth century sealed its fate. William of Tyre, chronicler of the First Crusade, saw no more than ruins.

It was not until 1806 that Jerash was rediscovered by a determined German scholar, Ulrich Jasper Seetzen. Other travellers followed and by the late nineteenth century the place was almost on a tourist trail: the Prince of Wales's sons were taken there in 1882. Under the Mandate the excavation and protection of Jerash was a high priority of the Department of Antiquities, and a great deal has been achieved by the Jordanian authorities in recent decades. The context of the site has been respected, although the modern town, where in 1878 the Ottomans settled considerable numbers of Circassians who had been displaced as a result of the war with Russia, has encroached upon most of the eastern section of the Roman city.

The visitor arrives from the south. The Triumphal Arch celebrating the visit of Hadrian serves as a frontispiece. Everything above the level of the central arch and the upper niches has been reconstructed, but the somewhat later lateral sections have not been reinstated. The exceptional width of the building was perfectly calculated to take full visual advantage of the rise this crowns. The architect evidently had a penchant for lavish decoration, and the acanthus bands at the bases of the engaged columns, although echoed on the South Gate of the city, are highly unusual. Between the arch and the South Gate, the road is flanked to the west by the hippodrome, a building that suffered severely in early times. The south-east side has now been partly reconstructed.

The South Gate, which is comparable with the Arch of Hadrian in detail and no doubt in date, opens to a short street leading through an arch to the Oval Piazza, past the temenos of the Temple of Zeus, which was dedicated in AD 166 under Geminius Marcianus – who was also responsible for the Temple of Hercules at Amman – and replaced earlier, and presumably less ambitious, temples to the deity. The magnificent north-east corridor of the temenos, entered from the street, is now used to show material found during the French excavation of the earlier shrine that stood in the northern section of the temenos and was demolished in AD 69–70: sections of columns applied with fluted plaster; fragments of painted mural schemes in red and yellow and a pale blue; and bits of partly pigmented moulded stucco. To reach the temple itself walk up to the left. On a substantial podium, the temple is hexastyle: the outer walls of the cella are relieved by a series of generous niches, while in the main room within there are thin pilasters.

West of the temple, built into the flank of the valley, is the South Theatre, begun under Domitian (81–96). The auditorium, with an unusual arrangement of circular recesses in the wall below the lower tier of benches, is relatively well preserved, even though the upper seats have been lost. And now that the restoration has had time to settle, this seems much less unsatisfactory than I at first thought it. The stage building also has been partly reconstructed. The view over the site from the upper seats more than makes up for a gnawing sense of disappointment with the theatre itself.

The Oval Piazza is one of the wonders of Jerash. This is not in fact oval: rather it has the shape of an inverted teardrop, and was brilliantly calculated to create a counterpart to the very much smaller curved piazzas within gates at both Palmyra and Bosra which served the specific function of preparing the visitor for the dramatic change of alignment between the approach road and the colonnaded cardo maximus that runs for some 823 metres/900 yards to the North Gate. The piazza, which dates from the first century AD, is framed by splendid Ionic colonnades, which have been sensitively reconstructed. The paving blocks are laid out in concentric rows.

Follow the cardo. Laid out in the first century and partly widened in the second, when Corinthian capitals replaced their Ionic predecessors, this was originally flanked by buildings and shops. The paving stones are laid diagonally, but with paired rows set from side to side at irregular intervals: in a number of places there is evidence of wear from wheeled traffic. The raised stretches of the pavement represent a Byzantine reconstruction. The first significant complex on the left is the macellum, or market. This has a central colonnaded hexagonal court round a fountain: there are exedras in the corners of the court and in that to the south-west a group of table supports of animal form. On the cardo north of the entrance to the macellum is a small fountain with a dedication to Julia Domna, the wife of Septimius Severus, who came from Emesa, now Homs, in Syria. Ahead is the south tetrapylon marking the junction with the south decumanus, a section of the colonnade of which has been reinstated: north of this are the scant foundations of a building of the Umayyad period, testifying to the final phase of civic life at Gerasa.

There follows the widest section of the cardo. A short way up on the left are the eight higher columns of the portico of the propylaeum of a temple, possibly dedicated to Dionysus, with a lavishly decorated central doorcase of the mid-second century. In the fourth century this structure was adapted as the gateway to the new cathedral, approached by a handsome flight of steps. Beyond the propylaeum, with pairs of yet taller columns, are the splendid remains of the late second-century nymphaeum, to make space for which the northern section of the propylaeum was rebuilt with the columns placed closer together. The recessed façade is in two tiers, with a particularly felicitous arrangement of niches and rectangular openings. It was originally pigmented, as a small area of paint in the upper niche on the left demonstrates. The large shallow basin in front of the building was a Byzantine introduction.

Further on, to the right, is the sixth-century Propylaeum Church, ingeniously inserted into a section of the original sacred route to the Temple of Artemis. Opposite this, flanked by shops on two floors, is the lavishly decorated propylaeum to the temple. The portal of this is of AD 150. The west elevation is equally impressive. Reconstructed steps lead steeply up to the terrace above, upon which there was an altar, part of the base of which is *in situ*. From the terrace further flights of stairs climbed to the large temenos, the colonnade of which is best preserved on the south side. Set back within this, on a tall podium, the Temple of Artemis

was the most conspicuous monument of Gerasa. Even now the approach is awe-inspiring. The temple may never have been completed, but the great Corinthian columns of the portico – all but one of the twelve are still in place – still stand majestically. Long exposure has enriched their colour, which thus contrasts with the pale tone of the lower sections of the columns of the temenos, which were buried until relatively recently. Theodosius's edict of 386 that pagan shrines could be destroyed was not taken too literally, but the entrance to the temple became a ceramic workshop in the Byzantine period. Now songbirds nest in the interstices of the columns.

From the temple cut north-west for the North Theatre, the back of which can already be seen. The theatre, which is smaller than its counterpart, had a strange charm in its tumbled state, but the restoration, completed in 1997, was not insensitive. A charming innovation of the design was the provision of trios of niches in the wall that backs the lower of the two tiers of benches. Names, presumably of proprietors or subscribers, on many of the benches are rather touching links with their original occupants. The theatre faces a row of four tall Corinthian columns, one of which has fallen, flanked by engaged columns attached to narrow piers, across the north decumanus. This intersects with the cardo at the North Tetrapylon. This handsome structure was, no doubt on account of its elegant coved vault, described as the Rotunda by the traveller James Silk Buckingham, who admits to acting in a way we would now consider reprehensible: 'I scrawled my name with the date, on the inner wall near where we sat' (*Travels among the Arab Tribes Inhabiting the Countries East of Syria and Palestine*, London, 1825).

By coincidence one of the very few buildings that cannot have changed much since Buckingham's time is just to the south-west of the tetrapylon, the West Baths. Shattered by time and encroached upon by vegetation,

The cardo maximus, with the propylaeum.

these seem to defy the modern town at their feet, which has long since engulfed the yet more ambitious East Baths.

The northern section of the cardo used to be particularly appealing. Here the original Ionic columns of the first century were not replaced. Fewer tourists come. Grass still grows among the paving stones. But as trees have been cleared away one is more aware of the proximity of the modern town; and although the North Gate has been splendidly reconstructed, recent building and relentless traffic mean that it is no longer much of a pleasure to look out across the valley towards Birketein, the place of the 'double pool' where the ancient Festival of Maiuma was held; there an appealing theatre, which originally had benches for 1,000 spectators, overlooks the cistern in which naked women were ritually immersed. A chorus of croaking frogs now competes with sounds from the main road. A path between trees leads to the picturesque ruin of the temple tomb of Germanus.

The early Christians did not approve of the Festival of Maiuma, yet after at least two endeavours to ban it, it was reinstated, albeit in purged form, in 535. While the Romans could adopt the gods of others, Christianity could only absorb the practices of earlier religions. Jerash became a Christian city; and not the least fascinating aspect of the place is the way in which Christianity came to impose its architectural presence. While the pilgrim to the Temple of Artemis climbed towards its great entrance portico, the Christian mounting the steps to the cathedral, passing the two pairs of Corinthian columns within the gate with bases on differing levels but aligned capitals which originally supported a bridge between now lost flanking colonnades, faced the cathedral's east end. Passages led round the cathedral, although that on the left was in time blocked by the construction of the south-west chapel, to the west front, with its three doorways. Little survives of the cathedral itself. But the Fountain Court to the west of this is more eloquent, although the Ionic colonnades that echoed the lost portico of the cathedral were largely demolished when the Basilica of St Theodore was built in 494–6, its apse projecting towards the fountain itself.

Before going to inspect the basilica, climb the steps to the north of the Fountain Court, known as the Sarapion Passage, to the Stepped Street, which climbed steeply from the cardo between the cathedral and the temenos of the Temple of Artemis. At the angle are the eroded remains of the baths built by Bishop Placcus in 454–5. Excavated in 1931, these serve to remind us how completely the church came to dominate every aspect of Byzantine life. One of Placcus' successors, Bishop Aeneas, initiated the construction of the basilica. From below it is the splendid lines of each of seven Corinthian columns that flanked the nave, seen above the austere polygonal base of the apse, that catch the eye. The basilica should be entered from the west through the screen of Ionic columns from the rectangular atrium. Unfortunately the visitor can no longer see the mosaics and marbles that adorned the church, or the arrangements which the excavators discovered in the little baptistery to the south of it. But it is fascinating to reflect that the bishops of Jerash sought deliberately to emulate the sequence of buildings associated with the Holy Sepulchre at Jerusalem, and ironic that the progression from the propylaeum to the basilica is now our best guide to the appearance of the structures that inspired these.

There are other, yet more ruinous, churches at Jerash. West of the basilica are three linked churches built between 529 and 533 and dedicated to Saints Cosmas and Damian, who were martyred at Cyrrhus in Syria, John the Baptist and George. The planning of these churches in a single rectangular block was evidently coordinated and the churches are set behind a colonnaded atrium. Many of the columns of this survive, as do the four recycled ones that originally supported the roof of the central church, that of the Baptist. The Church of Saints Cosmas and Damian is most notable for its figurative mosaics, which include representations of the donors, Theodore and Georgia, his wife, and an inscription recording that the church was dedicated in 533 under Bishop Paul. Mosaics were also found in the adjacent churches. The other churches of Jerash are of more specialized interest. To the west of the three churches, cut into the slope is what survives of the church founded by Bishop Genesius in 611, of basilica plan with a single apse. Further north, west of the Temple of Artemis, is the so-called Synagogue Church, originally a synagogue, which was adapted for Christian use under Bishop Paul in 530–1. Relatively little survives, but the pulvinated pedestals of the columns merit the slight detour. To the south, near the angle of the city wall, is the Church of Sts Peter and Paul, of about 540, founded by Bishop Anastasius. The mosaics, now covered up, were by the same team of craftsmen as those in the Church of St John. Near by is a stone marking the grave of G. Lankester Harding.

The small site museum is to the east of the cardo. Considering the scale of Roman Gerasa, the finds are somewhat disappointing. In the entrance there are two sections of a good Byzantine mosaic border, with heads at the corners and acanthus scrolls framing animals and a hunter. Further on there is a mosaic showing the city of Alexandria, with churches and other buildings within a wall studded with towers.

Jerash is very much on the tourist route. But a site that housed a population of 25,000 can well absorb coach parties by the dozen. And the sightseer who wanders to the fringes of the ancient city may still feel something of the sense of discovery that must have been experienced by tourists who visited Jerash before so many of the main monuments were excavated and restored.

5. QALAAT AR-RABADH

Qalaat ar-Rabadh, near Ajlun, which stands on a prominent spur looking out towards the valley of the Jordan, is the most impressive medieval Arab fortress in Jordan. It was built in 1184–5 by Izz ad-Din Usama, a cousin of Saladin, who had been the master of Aleppo and Damascus as well as Egypt since the death of Nur ad-Din in 1174. Saladin had long sought to drive the Crusaders from their kingdom of Jerusalem, and the construction of the castle can be seen as an element in his strategy, intended to prevent any possibility of renewed Frankish intervention east of the Jordan, and to answer the Crusaders' great fortress of Belvoir to the west of the river.

Saladin's decisive victory at Hattin in 1187 transformed the situation. But it did not diminish the importance of the castle. To the original core, roughly square in plan and with four towers, significant additions were made in 1214–15 by Aibak ibn Abdallah, who was in the service of the Caliph al-Malik al-Muazzam. These included a new entrance and the north-east bailey with two further towers. Despite the strength of the enlarged fortress and its splendid rock-cut fosse, ar-Rabadh fell to the Mongols in 1260 and was damaged. Recovered by the Mamelukes in the aftermath of their victory at 'Ain Jalut, the castle was restored, and apparently extended, under the immensely effective Sultan Baybars in 1262–3, as an inscription on the south-west tower attests. Subsequently ar-Rabadh was the base of a governor and, because of its position, an important post for both beacons and the celebrated carrier pigeon service that linked Cairo with Baghdad. Described as 'strong' by that most indefatigable of medieval pilgrim travellers Ibn Battuta, the castle was restored in 1927–9 and again in more recent years.

The approach is across the fosse, where a column of rock was left to

Qalaat ar-Rabadh from the south-east.

support a drawbridge. The entrance leads to an internal ramp that climbs to turn through a second gate, its arch decorated with crude carvings of birds – one single, two in combat – by the corner of one of the towers of 1214–5, and then turns again immediately to the left to a wider passage, a further turn to the right at the top of which represents the original entrance beside the eastern tower of Izz ad-Din Usama's fortress. To the left, arranged in two large rooms of the south tower, is the archaeological collection: the most beautiful of the exhibits is a group of Bronze Age lipped clay lamps, and there is also a Byzantine cross found at Mar Elias. Immediately outside, a door to the left leads to a gallery, the right wall of which was the southern side of the original fortress: from this one reaches a wider parallel room to the south. There are more galleries on the next level, the most impressive an L-shaped apartment above the museum with five embrasures for arrow slits, built of fine regular blocks and with a cornice on the external walls. But one's pleasure in this is sadly diminished by aggressive floor lights, which indeed mar the impact of the interior of much of the castle.

As Lankester Harding noted, the first phase of the building is characterized by rough masonry and narrow slits for windows, while the later openings are wider and 'sometime contained loose blocks which could be removed for light and air in times of peace'. Although partly bossed, the masonry is not of the calibre of that achieved in the great Crusader castles or of the somewhat later work of Saladin's son, al-Malik al-Zaher Ghazi, at Aleppo; and the castle is perhaps too well preserved to challenge the imagination. But its position is majestic. From afar it still dominates the landscape, despite recent building along the road up from Ajlun. The views to the west show why the site was chosen by Izz ad-Din Usama: on my penultimate visit the hills of Palestine were cast in haze, but Mount Hermon, crowned with fresh snow, hung in sharp focus to the north.

6. TELL MAR ELIAS

The recent papal visit to Jordan has drawn attention to the country's credentials as a place of Christian pilgrimage, as it undoubtedly was in the Byzantine era. The key sites are that of the Baptism beside the Jordan, Mar Elias, Mount Nebo, Machaerus and Lot's Cave. The Baptism site is a place to avoid: street lights all the way to the visitor centre, and then bussed tours on paths through tangled trees infested with flies to see vestigial Byzantine remains and look across the Jordan to bemused tourists on the Israeli-occupied West Bank, before taking in a rash of new churches, which in their turn may give future archaeologists rather a low view of our civilization.

Mar Elias, the birthplace of the prophet Elijah, is an altogether happier experience. There is a sign to the right by one of the hotels on the road up to Qalaat ar-Rabadh: after 1 kilometre turn left – there is no sign – and then, after 4 kilometres, right, just before a checkpoint. You see the hill on the left and there is a road up to the relatively discreet visitor centre.

To the right of the steps up to the hilltop there is a small church, with a smaller chapel, in a rock cutting. The main church on the summit, one of the mosaics in which is of 622, was of considerable size. Entered from the west – a cemented court overlies a well said to be 11 metres/36 feet deep – this was square with a single apse to the east, and further apses at the centres of the aisles. Little survives of the walls, but much of the mosaic flooring of the left aisle is intact, as is that of the two sacristies on either side of the main apse, that on the left decorated with grapes, its counterpart plain. To the west of the north aisle a door opened to the baptistery, which was at a lower level; the font is in place, as are the mosaics of the four sections of the room. To the south of the church were annexed buildings, some also with mosaics. Near by, steps lead down to a small necropolis with a lintel upon which a cross is painted in red.

But it is as much for the charm of the place and the shade of the evergreen oaks that Mar Elias merits the brief detour. There are tremendous views over the Ajlun hills and westwards to the valley of the Jordan. Dark cloud rolls in from the west. And if Mar Elias cannot be strictly proved to have been Elijah's birthplace, one can readily understand why the Byzantines believed that it was: it would have been an appropriate one.

7. PELLA: TABUQAT FAHL

Pella, near the village of Tabuqat Fahl, is beautifully placed on the flank of the hills to the east of the Jordan. An abundant natural spring has drawn successive waves of inhabitants to the site. This was occupied in the Neolithic period, and by the Middle Bronze Age (2200–1550 BC) had become a significant Canaanite city. In the fourteenth century BC Pihil was a trading partner and tributary of Egypt, as documents found at Tell Amarna attest. Conquered by the Neo-Babylonians in the sixth century BC, the place only revived in the Hellenistic era. Subsequently the city claimed to have been founded by Alexander, who had been born at Pella in Macedonia. Whether for this reason or because the name was a natural contraction of Pihil, the revived city was named Pella in the Seleucid period. Sacked in 83 BC by the Hasmonaean Alexander Jannaeus because it had failed to conform to Jewish observances, Pella was liberated from Jewish control by Pompey in 64 BC, to become part of the province of Syria. Roman rule saw a long period of prosperity at Pella, as in other cities of the Decapolis. Christianity first reached the city in AD 70 and became strongly entrenched in the following centuries. But Pella, now part of the province of Palestina Secunda, was apparently in decline even before the Arab victory over the Byzantines at Fahl, just west of the town, in 635. Earthquakes in 717 and 747 took their toll, but the place was not to be abandoned for several centuries. Subsequently the village of Tabuqat Fahl grew up on the site: this was moved to the west when serious excavation began.

The site is of considerable size, with a large partly artificial mound overlooked across the Wadi Jirm from the south by the bare Tell al-Husn. Approaching from the modern village, the road passes south

The Large Church from the east.

of the West Church, a few columns of the atrium of which have been put back in place: a substantial covered cistern formed part of the complex. The road then skirts the mound, but while I would probably choose to walk up to this from the lower entrance, some visitors make for the resthouse on higher ground to the east, from which there are wide views over the site.

Excavations over some thirty years by the Australians have revealed many layers of occupation on the tell at Pella: the substantial remains of an impressive Canaanite temple, built of outsize masonry; a major secular building west of this, overlying its Bronze Age predecessor; Iron Age domestic structures; a Roman gatehouse; Umayyad houses; and the lower section of a Mameluke mosque.

By far the most appealing monument of Pella is the Large Church of about 400. Of cathedral scale and raised on a platform terraced to the south, this was inserted in the centre of the Roman town, beside the ruinous odeon and a bath complex, and above the former forum near

the spring that had been the town's *raison d'être*. A monumental stairway leads up to the colonnaded court that served as narthex, but this was a seventh-century addition, as the court was originally entered from a passage between outsize columns on the north. The paving of the court is in contrasting reddish and white blocks: and while most of the reused columns are in a stone with a touch of red, the two flanking the former portal to the church are of a greenish veined marble. The central nave of the church is much wider than the aisles. The paving of the left aisle is well preserved, as is the seating arrangement in the apse. But it is inevitably the Corinthian columns, ten on either side of the nave, that hold the eye.

Higher up and behind the Large Church is the smaller East Church, its apse cut into the hillside. This too was entered through a colonnaded atrium. Within the church there were two columns at either side, of a yellow marble flecked with red, and four rows of benches for clergy in the apse; a beautiful Byzantine acanthus capital hints at the refinement of the building.

Many of the discoveries that have been made at Pella are of most interest to the specialist. But it would be difficult to be indifferent to the magic of the site in the late afternoon as shadows lengthen. The more energetic may be tempted to make up to the summit of tomb-riddled Tell al-Husn, where there are traces of Early Bronze Age and late Roman fortifications. Others may prefer to linger near the church, as I did briefly on a December Friday: youths filled cans of water at the spring, and beyond perhaps forty people had gathered in five or six circles picnicking on the grass, as the light gradually drained. They had, I knew, come less for what the archaeologists have revealed of ancient Pella than because of the beauty of its setting.

The Large Church from the south-west.

8. GADARA: UMM QAIS

Less ancient than neighbouring Pella, Gadara has more to offer to the sightseer. The city, as such, was founded in the Hellenistic period, and was initially in the sphere of the Ptolemies, from whom it was taken by Antiochus III in 218 BC. Like Pella, Gadara fell to the Hasmonaean Alexander Jannaeus, only to become part of Pompey's province of Syria in 64 BC. One of Pompey's key associates, Demetrius, came from Gadara, which as a result benefited notably from his rule, Josephus going so far as to say that he refounded it. This may in part explain Octavian's decision of 30 BC, after his victory at Actium, to award Gadara to King Herod the Great of Judea. The Gadarenes petitioned unsuccessfully against this, but it was only after the king's death in AD 4 that Gadara returned to Roman rule. Once again in the province of Syria, Gadara was one of the cities of the Decapolis.

It was at Gadara that, as St Matthew records, Christ cured two possessed men whose demons caused a herd of swine to charge down a steep bank and drown, presumably in the Yarmuk. Gadara's period of high prosperity was in the second century, as the major extant monuments attest. The city had a distinguished intellectual tradition, which may have contributed to its resistance to Herodian rule, and this was maintained under the Romans: the philosopher Philodemus, who came from Gadara, was a friend of both Virgil and Horace, while the Emperor Tiberius was taught the art of rhetoric by a Gadarene orator, Theodorus. Gadara had a bishop as early as 325 and continued to flourish under Umayyad rule. The earthquakes of 717 and 747 took their toll, but the site continued to be occupied during the medieval era. In the late nineteenth century, partly as a result of immigration from Samaria, the village of Umm Qais developed on the former acropolis. That the ruins represented the historic Gadara was first recognized by Seetzen on his journey of 1806.

On the way up from the modern town, the road passes two impressive underground tombs, those of the Germani and of Lucius Sentius Modestus, both with splendid basalt doors carved with fictive panels and, in the case of the latter, a central vertical locking bar. Gadara is now entered from the ticket office at the south side of the acropolis, the walls of which are best seen from the car park. The main path strikes north towards the impressive second-century West Theatre, of black basalt, much of which survives because it was built against the side of the acropolis hill. The lower section of the auditorium is substantially intact, the upper, thirteenth, row with individually cut high-backed seats rather than benches: the second tier is of nine rows, but only loose blocks from the upper level survive. Blue irises somehow grow in the interstices of the blocks. The barrel-vaulted passages beneath the auditorium are particularly impressive, and part of the stage building is in place.

From the top of the theatre there is a good view of the so-called Basilica Terrace to the north, excavated on the eastern side into the natural rock, which takes its name from a major fifth- or sixth-century church, in front of which the footings of a smaller church can be seen. To get to this, leave by the passage at the north end of the lower tier of seats. The basilica was a sophisticated example of the Byzantine fascination with spatial forms: externally square yet internally an octagon, evidently surmounted by a dome, supported on eight Corinthian columns and the massive corner piers. Much of the patterned paving survives, and the eight columns of the west portico have been reinstated. To the north of the basilica is a large court, with limestone Corinthian columns and a fine pavement of white and reddish stone.

Steps lead down to the decumanus, and afford a splendid view of one of the more refined buildings of Gadara, the nymphaeum, built surely as much for effect as for any practical use. Much has gone, but the rhythm of what survives is impressive: the basalt was offset by a splendid white frieze and by sculpture, of which a statue of a girl from what was evidently a larger group is in the museum. At this point in the circuit of the city there are two options: the more tempting no doubt would be to head westwards along the spectacular stretch of the street and then to return to the museum; but there is also a case for turning east, to see the large artificial terrace laid out on the north side of the hill in the second century BC for a temple: nothing significant survives of the temenos, but the stump of the podium of the cella remains, with three internal rooms. On the opposite, south, side of the decumanus is the much robbed North Theatre. Part of the stage building has been excavated and substantial sections of the internal corridors and ramps are accessible. There are intriguing differences between the masonry of these and their better preserved counterparts in the West Theatre: there in the walls, as opposed to the vaults, above each course or two courses of large blocks, are narrower courses, while in the North Theatre the courses are all of uniform large blocks.

From below the North Theatre one can now follow the length of the decumanus. Because of the nature of the site, this runs not through the centre of the city but just within the northern alignment of the city wall. Much of the original paving survives, rutted in places by wheels, and evidence of a sophisticated drainage system has been found. Many of the columns of the flanking colonnades have been put back in place, and others remain where they fell. In the eastern section the basalt paving stones are laid diagonally; by the nymphaeum this changes, and they are laid in rows from side to side.

The decumanus runs westwards from the nymphaeum for roughly a kilometre/0.6 miles. In the first block on the left is an early fourth-century bath complex, best preserved on the opposite, southern, side. A little further on, to the right, is what survives of a late second-century building

The West Theatre.

of considerable refinement, formerly identified as a nymphaeum and now described as the Podium Monument. Some way beyond this, also to the north of the road, is the footprint of a semicircular church. The next significant building on the left, fronted by tall Corinthian columns, was a temple. Near this the paving of the street reverts to its earlier diagonal arrangement.

Beyond this, also to the south of the decumanus, was another major Christian complex, flanked by shops opening on to the street. Nearest to the road was a centrally planed church, the hexagonal pavement of which is startlingly white in the sunlight. Behind this was a large colonnaded court, with Corinthian columns of limestone, on the other side of which is the lateral colonnade, Ionic and of basalt, of a further church, much of which survives. This too was an octagon within a square, with circular apses in the corners: much of the grey-veined white marble paving is in place, as are the footings of the choir. Further on, also on the left, preceded by a circular structure of which only the foundations survive, is the subterranean Roman mausoleum that may have been used for the tomb of Zacharias, who was martyred at Gadara in AD 303. Only such a function can explain the subsequent decision to place the apse of a large basilica above this, and to make elaborate arrangements for access to the mausoleum. Little survives of the superstructure of the basilica itself, but the plan of this was established in 1998: the scale of the church has led to the suggestion that it celebrated Christ's healing of the possessed men. To the west was a large colonnaded court, now an olive grove.

The decumanus continues to the West Gate, of which relatively little was left for the archaeologists to disinter. Outside this on the same alignment, the road, now metalled, continues, passing the jumbled remains of a hippodrome to the foundations of the Roman monumental gate from which those approaching from the west would have had their first full view of the city.

Return along the decumanus to the nymphaeum and turn right to see the row of twenty barrel-vaulted shops — for commerce was as vital to ancient cities as it is to our own — under the Basilica Terrace. Six of the basalt façades are in place; and the doorcases are handled with great elegance, as is most evident at midday when the sunlight defines their crisp detail. The West Theatre too benefits from afternoon light.

On the east side of the acropolis, most conveniently reached by walking up the steps from the Basilica Terrace past the Rest House, is the site museum, in Beit Rusan, the most prominent house of the Ottoman village. The most substantial of the finds is an outsize but headless statue, most probably of Tyche, patroness of the city under the Seleucids, whose cult was maintained elsewhere in the Near East under Rome. The majority of the collection is laid out in the courtyard, but some of the smaller sculptures are in a room that you may need to have unlocked: the most memorable object is a coiled snake, with well-observed scales. At the museum it is possible to ask to see the section of an aqueduct, the Qanawat al-Far'aoun, cut into the chalk below the acropolis. This dates from Hellenistic or early Roman times and was still thought sufficiently remarkable to be mentioned in the tenth century by the Iranian writer Hamza al-Isfahani.

The buildings of the abandoned village on the acropolis tell their own tale: pillage. Gates are built of column drums and crowned with upturned bases and querns. There are appropriated lintels and basalt blocks. And here one can well imagine the Gadarene swine charging to destruction, when looking across to the Golan, its southern spurs fluttering like a yellow Fortuny skirt laid out in the sunlight, and the land falling away towards the Lake of Tiberias below it to the west.

9. AL-HABIS

Al-Habis is for very obvious reasons among the least-visited sights in Jordan. The caves in cliffs high above the river Yarmuk literally overhang the Syrian frontier and tourism is not encouraged. When the caves were first occupied is not clear. They were evidently known to the Byzantines; and the plain vault of the so-called Church Cave has been seen as evidence that this was used in the Iconoclastic period, and thus most probably in the eighth century. The Crusaders in their initial period of expansion, early in the twelfth century, and with their genius for identifying strategic positions, saw the potential of the caves and clearly expanded the network of excavations. Cava de Suet, as they named this most unusual of fortifications, had the potential not only to disrupt communication between Damascus and the Arabs of the hinterland, but also to defend the kingdom of Jerusalem from attack. The chronicler of the First Crusade William of Tyre records a spirited counterattack after the caves had been seized by a raiding party of seventy infidels. The Crusaders, versed in the use of mines during sieges, adopted the reverse course and began digging from above: it took three weeks for the defendants to submit. It must be admitted that there is no visual evidence to support the chronicler's account.

To approach the site from Gadara, take the road to Irbid. After some 15 kilometres/9½ miles, a road comes in from the left. Turn, follow this past the approach to Abila, and further on fork right for Hartha, 3 kilometres ahead. Cross the roundabout and continue for 4 kilometres on the Aqraba road. This descends to a narrow valley planted with olives, and then turns to the left before a checkpoint. As it turns, a track leads

Al-Habis.

off to the right. Park and walk to the end of the valley, and look out over the Wadi Habis, which plunges down to the Yarmuk. The caves can be seen in a cliff face high on the escarpment to the right: an obvious path leads to them.

The lowest of the caves are not of particular interest, with the exception of the Church Cave itself. This was cruciform and had a vaulted ceiling; there are two small recesses near the entrance. The upper levels of the fortress are now inaccessible without appropriate equipment. The sounds of a pump rise from the valley floor. The setting is by any standard spectacular, with the land falling away dramatically to the river and Syria stretched out at one's feet.

When I first tried to go, red flags signalled that it would be tactless to do so; and three men in a van, who may or may not have been following me, warned that I might be shot at from either side. More recently a soldier urged caution. Yet families picnic among the olive trees near the road and on the much more exposed outcrop above the track. Footings cut into the rock show that there was once a small settlement here, and there are no fewer than four game boards, each of two rows of six holes with a larger one on each side, within a few feet of each other on the saddle.

10. ABILA: QUWEILBEH

Abila is, with its more battered neighbour to the south Capitolas, one of the less visited cities of the Decapolis. Of course, the ruins cannot compete with those of Jerash, or claim the Christian associations of Gadara. But they are visually more compelling than those of Pella, and the setting has an untrammelled charm.

The site straddles two hills, Tell Abil and Khirbet Umm al-Amad to the west of the Wadi Quweilbeh, and has been occupied, at least intermittently, since Neolithic times, for water is abundant and the surrounding territory fertile. Appropriately enough the name Abila means 'meadow', 'lush' or 'green' in Hebrew. The Hellenistic town grew up on the tell, and faint traces of its walls can be made out. Pompey's imposition of Roman rule evidently heralded a long period of prosperity. The city is first mentioned by the second-century geographer Claudius Ptolemy, in his account of the Decapolis. Like other Byzantine towns in the area, Abila seems to have made the transition to Umayyad rule relatively easily, but it is likely that the earthquake of 746 had a devastating effect on the urban economy. The site was eventually abandoned in the medieval period. When Seetzen with some difficulty found his way to Abila in 1806, hotfoot from Gadara and as he did not as yet know on his way to Jerash, it was wholly deserted; he commented on arches and columns among the ruins. Happily the place is still deserted – although a large chicken farm has recently been built across the wadi – and what the archaeologists have resurrected has been achieved with tact.

Unlike Pella and Gadara, Abila is not marked on most maps. It can be approached from Gadara or Irbid, by taking the road to the former from the last, but after some 7 kilometres/4½ miles at a left turn marked to Umm Qais (20 kilometres) continue ahead for 7 kilometres to a left turn to Hartha. Shortly afterwards columns on Khirbet Umm al-Amad ('mother of the columns') can be seen: the road descends after a kilometre to Ain Quweilbeh, the spring from which the stream of the name flows. If you are not short of time, the spring, now imprisoned in concrete, is the best place from which to set out on a circuit of the ruins. The alternative is to turn right from the Hartha road and park by the columns.

Tombs are cut into both sides of the valley. The more interesting are on the right flank, but, if only to increase the chance of finding the guardian with the keys to some of these, it makes sense to explore those on the left first. Excavated from the rock, many of these include small *loculi* for individual burials. Cut up the slope to make for the Byzantine basilica on the level summit of Khirbet Umm al-Amad, so named from the columns of the church, which was excavated in 1984–90. The lower courses of the structure have been consolidated, and the rows of recycled columns, alternately of granite and – as Seetzen observed – basalt, which separated the nave from the aisles have been partly re-erected. Keeping to the high ground, go on to Tell Abil, where much work has recently been done. A section of the foundations of the defensive walls can be made out on the approach. At the top of the tell there was a second basilica, constructed of large pillaged basalt and limestone blocks, no doubt replacing a pagan temple, from which a statue of Diana found near by may have come.

Between the two hills is a saddle from which a splendid stretch of Byzantine road descends. This was surfaced in basalt, and many of the paving stones were carefully scored to reduce the risk of slipping. On the right, cut into the side of the southern hill, is the unmistakable form of the cavea of a substantial theatre, into which the Umayyads inserted a small fortress. Opposite this, built against the side of Tell Abil, was a bath complex. To the north-east of this is a remarkable cruciform basilica, by far the most ambitious of the churches of Byzantine Abila, and of which

The basilica below the acropolis.

the columns have recently been most successfully re-erected. There were five doors on the west wall, an arrangement found at Suweida and elsewhere in Syria, and the nave and inner aisles were flanked by four rows of columns. All but two of the columns are of basalt and, a single Corinthian example apart, the capitals are all Ionic. Much of the marble floor is in place. The principal apse projects from the back wall and smaller apses are built out from the eastern ends of the side walls.

Below the church is the bridge over the wadi, a single arch a good 4.5 metres/15 feet below the level of the road above, part of the paving of which is *in situ*. You may be the only tourist, but you will not be alone. There are usually herdsmen with their flocks, wary dogs watching, tents below. On my second visit I was anxious to find the guardian. Eventually he materialized, handsome and helpful, and we made the usual exchange of names as we walked up the east flank of the wadi. The 'Arab frescoes', as monolingual Ali termed them, are of Roman date. These have for the most part suffered from damp. The first of the painted tombs has a quite consequential entrance; the others are literally holes in the hillside, through which one crawls or clambers as may be: the build-up of mud and stones on the protective metal doors showed that there were not many visitors. The ceilings, where they have not fallen in, are divided into small compartments with decorative motifs. More rewarding are the murals on the walls, with birds, dolphins, heads of women, flowers, a frieze of grapes and so forth. In the third of the tombs that are shown, with an elaborate *trompe l'oeil* decorative scheme, the spandrels of the arch opposite the entrance are painted with two cockerels. A little further on, lower down the slope, is another painted tomb, the basalt door of which has a fictive bar and lock. There are murals of figures, including the upper half of a woman holding a tablet, painted in near grisaille, ochre and pale brown, which shows how accomplished the 'Abila School' could be; near by, less well preserved, is a compartment with a bird among rushes. I rather overtipped Ali, but he had gone beyond the call of duty on a cold

December afternoon, and enabled me to imagine, if only for the moment, that I might begin to comprehend something of the world of Abila's long-dead worthies. Revisiting the tombs more recently after heavy rain, I was uncomfortably aware of the conservation problems these present.

The Byzantine road: grooved paving stone.

11. QASR AL-HALLABAT

While many of the desert castles for which Jordan is justly celebrated were new foundations, the Umayyads knew well how to exploit the buildings they found throughout the former provinces of Byzantine Syria. This process of efficient assimilation and architectural emulation is well expressed at Qasr al-Hallabat.

Placed on a low hill near the natural frontier between the steppe to the west, much of which was habitable, and the desert, at a point where the basalt thrown up by the extinct volcanoes of the Jebel al-Arab, beyond the Syrian border, meets the less hospitable chert, this was one of a number of forts intended to monitor the territory between the Via Nova Traiana and the oasis of Azraq.

The first Roman fort, relatively modest in size, was at the north-west corner of the later structure and may have been built in the reign of Marcus Aurelius (161–80). It was enlarged under Caracalla (212–15), as an inscription implies, to conform in plan with countless other such forts, square with projecting angle towers. An inscription of 529, which may, however, have been brought from elsewhere, implies that work was done in the time of the Emperor Justinian, who directed vast resources to the defences of Syria against the Persian enemy. Much more significant was the intervention of the Umayyads, who substantially reconstructed what they found. It is to them that we owe the striking combination in the outer walls of a mellow yellowish limestone and courses of basalt. The Umayyads remodelled the interior structures, building both in basalt and in limestone. The gate on the east leads to an L-shaped court. On the right there is an elegantly carved well head, near a door surmounted by

Qasr al-Hallabat from the reservoir.

a window, which opens to a large chamber: to the left of this is a smaller room with a damaged mosaic of birds among trees. In the block behind this is a court with a mosaic of a simple diagonal design: there are low benches round the walls and at the south end a triple arcade, two sections of which are also floored in mosaic. Of the rooms in the south range, one beside the south-east corner tower is of particular interest because a considerable number of blocks inscribed with a decree of the Emperor Anastasius (491–518) were set in the walls; others, found elsewhere by the excavators, are now in the visitor centre. Neither strictly a fortress nor really a palace as we would understand the term, the qasr testifies to the sophisticated standards to which the Umayyads had become accustomed, and perhaps also to their peripatetic instincts.

To the south-east is a mosque, probably of the eighth century. This has been impeccably restored by the Spanish team which has so greatly added to our understanding of the whole complex. On the flanks of the

hill were a number of lesser buildings of the Umayyad period, many of which have also now been excavated. To the south and west the hill is skirted by a wadi, which is dry except after winter rains. Almost due south of the qasr is a large ten-sided but roughly triangular reservoir, some of the blocks of the walls of which are of impressive size: this was fed by a channel from the south. To the north ancient field systems have been recorded and dams were built at intervals across the wadi bed to retain flood water. Three kilometres/2 miles to the south is an appealing bath building of the Umayyad period, the Hammam as-Sarah: this also has recently been restored.

12. UMM AL-JIMAL

Bosra to the north, now in Syria, was the metropolis to which the Roman and Byzantine inhabitants of the territory of northern Jordan east of Mafraq would most naturally have related. The Via Nova Traiana, the key defensive artery laid out under the Emperor Trajan after AD 106, ran from there to Azraq. A fine paved section of this crosses a modern road on the outskirts of the village of Ba'ij: the best approach is by way of Zubeidiyeh, reached from the outskirts of Mafraq by a turn to the right off the main road to the border. In Ba'ij fork right for Umm al-Jimal ('mother of camels'), which is incontestably the most atmospheric late Roman site in Jordan. Here to a remarkable extent we can sense the rhythms of life not in a mere cluster of early houses, as is the case in so many of the so-called 'dead cities' of northern Syria, but in a small town.

Not apparently named in early sources, or identified in any inscription found on the site, Umm al-Jimal may, as inscriptions on blocks that were later reused imply, have been occupied while the Nabataeans controlled the area. The town, however, grew during the Roman period. A fort was laid out in about AD 300 and incorporated within the town wall. The inhabitants did not aspire to any Hippodamian plan, laid out with regular intersecting streets. Their houses and other buildings are grouped in clusters, and it was the security requirements of these that determined the line of the town wall. The place's heyday was in the sixth century, to which many, indeed most, of the extant buildings belong, when here as in the Hauran to the north there was a thriving agricultural economy and the financial strain of the Byzantines' long struggle with Persia had not as yet been fully felt. A population estimated at between six and eight thousand was served by at least fourteen churches. Umm al-Jimal contracted after the Arab conquest, and did not survive the earthquakes of the eighth century. Thereafter the site was abandoned for over a millennium. Although a few buildings were repaired by the Druze, who had occupied the Hauran in the nineteenth century, Umm al-Jimal was largely untouched in 1918, when T. E. Lawrence saw it. He considered that 'such incongruous buildings, in what was then and now a desert cockpit, accused their builders of insensitivity' and that these 'disclosed a prosaic blindness to the transience of politics', which was at once 'aggressive and impudent'.

Umm al-Jimal rises from the plain in black silhouette. Most visitors arrive from the south, by a road off the main highway to the east, and the modern visitor centre is to the south of the ruins. But the Roman or Byzantine visitor would have approached from Ba'ij on a side road from the Via Nova Traiana, entering the town by the West, or Commodus, Gate; and – for those with time – this remains the logical point from which to begin, even though it now entails crossing the site. Just outside the gate is the sixth-century West Church, the arcade between the nave and south arcade of which still bears much of the clerestory above. The gate itself was originally built between AD 177 and 180, by when a considerable civic settlement had grown up.

Some 183 metres/200 yards south of the gate is the rather well-preserved so-called praetorium. The masonry is of a high order, with a central door opening to a courtyard which originally had four columns, presumably to support a superstructure; to the right of this is a fine cruciform room, the barrel vaults of the arched projections supporting a cornice for the lost corbelled ceiling, the Druze replacement of which has in turn collapsed. In 411–12 the barracks, some 183 metres/200 yards south-west of the praetorium and near the official entrance to the site, with its two towers, seems to have taken on the role of the earlier fort. The main gate, the basalt door of which has fallen, is on the east and

Umm al-Jimal: the West Church.

Umm al-Jimal: the barracks.

opens to a large courtyard. The projections from the upper windows of the six-storeyed south-east tower are, or were, marked with crosses and the names of the four archangels: the cross is also found on a lintel.

Christianity took a deep hold on the town. The cathedral, east of the praetorium, was built in 556, but incorporates as a lintel an inscription referring to the joint rule of Valens, Valentian and Gratian in AD 371. It has now been cleared, to reveal the bases of the square piers which supported the arches dividing the nave from the aisles, fragments of the mosaic of the nave with a scrolling vine pattern, and the base of the screen to the choir, as well as the seating arrangement in the apse where the bishop's place was three levels higher than that of the other clergy. Some of the other churches were associated with specific groups of houses. Not the least of the pleasures of Umm al-Jimal is to lose oneself among these, and sense something of the claustrophobic urban character of the Byzantine town. In the south-west corner a series of houses were set against the wall. In that variously numbered I and VI (Butler) is a block with dedications in both Nabataean and Greek. Further on, set between three houses, is the South-west Church. The basalt masonry of the houses varies in quality. The main walls were carefully faced in regular courses on both sides, and smaller stones were inserted between the facing blocks. Corbelling was used to support the roofing blocks, for wood was at a premium in this harsh environment. The technique is well demonstrated in the group of houses that back on to the wall, east of the South-west Church. Some of the more rewarding houses are in the cluster to the north of these, notably number 49, more regular in plan than its neighbours, and which incorporates part of an earlier structure: off the courtyard are two rooms intended for animals, in one of which there is a row of mangers.

A rather larger group of houses lies to the east of the barracks, extending to the line of the wall and backing on to the lane that led to the East Gate. Just within this is the large so-called Sheikh's House. The masonry is particularly fine, and two of the door lintels were ingeniously strengthened, one with a relieving arch, the other by a small window above; high up a column separates two arched windows of a room on the second floor. Making for the cathedral, one passes a number of substantial houses, all with at least one cistern, and most with provision for animals. Near by is the Double Church, the northern component of which is the better preserved.

There is much of interest in the northern area of the town. Just beyond the cluster of houses north of the East Gate is the poorly preserved rectangular Roman fort. By the south-west corner of this there is a large rectangular reservoir, somewhat disfigured by relatively modern plaster. This was fed by a channel from the main aqueduct, which brought water from higher ground to the north-east. In the fort itself some walls have been cleared, and there is a cistern, fed by a channel from the same aqueduct, the line of which can be seen. The East Gate of the fort, in effect the north-east gate of the town, is still impressive. Further north, at the angle of the town wall, is the North-east Church, of basilica form, still in legible condition, and with a small room off the south aisle that retains its original roof. This was balanced at the north-eastern corner of the enclosure by the less well preserved North Church. Between the churches and just within the wall are two partly rock-cut cisterns, smaller and less regular than the reservoir by the fort. These were also fed from the aqueduct, and would have been used by the inhabitants of the irregular triangle of buildings immediately to the south. Among the houses is the large but very ruinous Julianos Church, and near by, some 100 metres/109 yards from the West Gate, the Claudianus Church with an inscribed lintel bearing a cross.

The centre of the modern village is to the north-west, but this has spread in recent years, rather to the detriment of the ruins. And now that they are fenced off, sheep no longer graze among the tumbled houses and no women in flowing headdresses chatter beside the fort, while their children play noisily out of sight. To understand this aspect of Umm al-Jimal as it was, one must now go to Umm as-Sarub, 7 kilometres/4½ miles beyond Ba'ij, where the village takes no notice of the fence and a donkey is happily tethered outside the central door of the Church of Saints Sergius and Bacchus, to which a tapering minaret was added when it was converted as a mosque.

But life has returned to the basalt plain. The wide views across this help to explain why Rome planted its fortress at Umm al-Jimal, but in the heat of the summer the garrison must have envied the inhabitants of the more temperate Jebel al-Arab, which in the winter can clearly be seen to the north. The miracle of the place is that the unyielding basalt walls make it possible for us to sense something of the pattern of urban life on the very margin of the Byzantine Empire.

13. DEIR AL-KAHF

The stretch of basalt desert to the east of Umm al-Jimal, the southern section of the Hauran, the Roman Auranitis, was occupied in Roman times and has in recent decades once more come to support a settled population. This has obscured the evidence of early agriculture disclosed by early aerial photographs, and changed the context of the Roman fort at Deir al-Kahf some 26 kilometres/16 miles further east. It is possible that this is the base of Speluncae recorded in the Notitia Dignitatum, the fullest surviving record of roads and place names throughout the Empire. The fort, which was built in AD 306, as an inscription that has now been lost established, and which needed further attention between 367 and 375, was approximately equidistant between the legionary bases at Bosra and Azrak, and just to the east of the road linking these and running northwards along the east flank of the Jebel al-Arab towards Damascus. The road is thought to have been laid out in 208–10 and subsequently served as an extension to the Strata Diocletiana, the military road from Sura on the Euphrates by way of Palmyra to Damascus, on which the defence of Syria depended. More specifically the fort and its smaller and less well preserved neighbour at Deir al-Khin protected the southern flank of the Hauran.

A photograph published by Father Poidebard in 1934 shows the building in splendid isolation. Now this has been encroached upon by a modern village. But the basalt walls are substantially intact. Towers originally of three storeys with corbelled floors and roofs project at three corners and in the centres of the north and western walls: on my visit children clambered over the best-preserved tower, gratified to have a new audience. I entered by a late gate in the west wall, dignified by a pair of recycled basalt pilasters and capitals. The original gate, the tip of the basalt door of which emerges from the ground, was at the centre of the east wall. Ranges on two storeys lined the interior walls. It has been calculated that these would have accommodated a force of four or five hundred soldiers and a smaller number of horses. The main cistern was reached by a subsidiary door by the south-west tower, and is now filled with fallen masonry, including column drums and a crude capital. The fort was maintained in the Byzantine era, when a church was built in the courtyard opposite the gate.

The Roman fort at Deir al-Kahf.

14. JAWA

The Roman and Byzantine sites of the basalt desert represent a world we
almost understand, a world ruled by emperors whose names are more
or less familiar to us and in which religions we can identify prevailed. Jawa
is only 8 kilometres/5 miles beyond Deir al-Khin. But here we are in a
wholly different world, a world we can only judge from the evidence of
basalt walls and water catchment, a world that has left no historic record.
Here, for a brief half century during the Chalcolithic period in the fourth
millennium BC, a people who have left no other trace were able to sustain
a surprisingly sophisticated city in what must in every sense have been a
hostile terrain that had never before supported a settled population. First
revealed by an aerial photograph taken by Poidebard, Jawa was excavated
between 1972 and 1975 by S. W. Helms: his *Jawa: Lost City of the Black
Desert* (London, 1981) gives a vivid account of the site.

A rough track leads from a group of farms. Jawa at length appears as
a black crest on an outcrop that rises above two branches of the Wadi
Rajil. The builders of Jawa, who may have been refugees from elsewhere,
realized that they could harness the water that flowed in the wadi after
the winter rains. They knew that any dams across the main stream would
be broken by flash floods and therefore they built up an elaborate system
of water deflection, with a total of some 8 kilometres/5 miles of channels
that directed water to a series of reservoirs in the subsidiary wadi. These
made it possible to support a sizeable town, which developed in two
phases. The earlier, the upper town, was protected by a formidable wall.
This was of basalt and roughly lozenge-shaped in plan, with seven gates,
the most imposing of which is near the middle of the west wall. Near the
centre of the plateau of scattered basalt blocks that represents the upper
town is the so-called citadel, constructed in roughly 1000 BC, when the

Wall of the upper town.

site was briefly reoccupied; in addition to the outer walls, lintels and some internal divisions can be made out. The lower town, built on the sloping flanks of the outcrop, was enclosed by a second, but less formidable, defensive wall.

The three main reservoirs were below the town to the west. That one of these has been appropriated for a modern irrigation system shows how judicious the inhabitants of Jawa were in the manner in which they shaped their environment. But their success in doing so came at a price. The water they had saved drew others to Jawa, and eventually, despite the sophistication of their defensive walls, the inhabitants of the city were overwhelmed. Their hydrological skills went with them.

I lingered under darkening cloud, and at length set back along the track. I had walked for a mile when I heard an engine. The farmer by whose house I had left my car had sent his son to collect me, and I knew that it would be impossible to evade his hospitable invitation. The women were ordered from the large reception room even before we got to the anteroom: coffee appeared, then a large bowl of water, and finally tea. The television masked my total conversational inadequacy: we graduated from an American soap opera, by way of a local pop star, to the news, with tragically graphic clips of Palestinian girls who had been shot by Israeli soldiers. For the creators of Jawa were by no means the last people in the Near East to be driven from what they had come to regard as their land.

15. QASR BURQU

Qasr Burqu is one of the most haunting sites in Jordan, lost in the desert east of the Jebel al-Arab. Even now it takes both time and a degree of effort to get there. The nearest hotels for the visitor are at Azraq, some 174 kilometres/108 miles from Ruwayshid, where not trusting my hireling or its tyres, I asked in the main street for a taxi: within minutes a helpful man had asked two youths, Muhammed and Ali, to take me to the qasr and arranged terms. The track is signed from the main road: much of it is over hard sand, both golden and red, but after rain there were hazards even for a four-wheel-drive Datsun handled by a determined Bedouin. So progress at times was slow, and 20 kilometres/12½ miles seemed a long distance. At length the shadow of the shattered tower

The tower from the south-east.

could be seen, rising above the contour of the basalt, and we edged our way through this until I suggested it would be easier to walk.

At Burqu as at Jawa, permanent settlement was made possible by the control of water. Jawa failed within a few generations. By contrast Burqu was inhabited, at least intermittently, for over a millennium. But we do not know why the Romans, if indeed it was they, built the dam that created the lake at Burqu. For this was well beyond their frontier. Perhaps they had some such arrangement as later existed with the Ghassanids on the fringe of the Jebel al-Arab. In any case the original tower was no doubt built to protect the water that must have been a considerable asset to those who used this. Further buildings may have been added in the Byzantine era, when Burqu may have become a monastery. But much of what can now be seen was evidently due to the Amir al-Walid, subsequently caliph from 705 until 715, as an inscription of 700 attested.

Burqu with the lake.

The dam is at the north end of the lake, the qasr near the lake's southern tip. The walls enclose an area that was roughly square. The entrance was on the north. Rooms were ranged against the eastern and south walls. In the middle of the east range was an unusual small apsed room, alternatively interpreted as a hall and a chapel. The circular room in the south range, which may have been built earlier than that which flanks it, is presumably of Byzantine date, as otherwise the cross on the lintel would be difficult to explain. The tower is clearly of a much more refined build than the other structures, with nineteen courses of carefully graded stones below a row that projects slightly, above which are a further fifteen. There is a small door, now choked with masonry, on the west side facing the lake. On the east, much of the masonry has both fallen into the body of the building and cascaded outwards, so one can walk up the jumble of fallen blocks to gain some sense of the scale of the three internal rooms. Presiding as it still does over the Byzantine and Umayyad buildings that cluster round it, the shattered tower at Burqu is, like the artificial lake in which it is reflected, a strangely touching statement of human enterprise. And it is for this reason, rather than for any particular architectural qualities, that it is abundantly worth making the effort to go to Burqu. One can only hope that the future holds no visitor centre in store.

16. AZRAQ

'Then the blue fort on its rock above the rustling palms, with the fresh meadows and shining springs of water, broke on our sight.' Alas, things have changed since 1917, when T. E. Lawrence established his headquarters at Azraq. The Roman fort, black rather than blue, is now fringed by modern buildings. Traffic has long since dispelled the 'unfathomable silence' that Lawrence recalled. And although the oasis at Azraq is even now a remarkable phenomenon, where one is still very conscious of the distinction between the desert and the sown, this is only because of heroic attempts in recent years to redress the catastrophic damage done by excessive water extraction.

The oasis was occupied in Palaeolithic times; and the strategic importance of its position at the head of the Wadi Sirhan – a significant route from the south – was evidently understood by the Romans. For they recognized that Azrak was a key to the protection of Syria, the Hauran and the prosperous cities of the Decapolis from any enemy who sought to cross the desert. The Strata Diocletiana, linking Azraq with Bosra and the chain of fortresses that marked the frontier, took its definitive form under Diocletian (284–305), and the oldest inscription found in the fort is of the period (from 286) when he and Maximian were co-Emperors. But while not necessarily the first Roman camp on the site, the fort may well have been begun earlier, as the satellite forts at Aseikhin to the north-east and Uweinid to the south-west were occupied in the third century. Commanding the 'shining springs' to the south, Azraq – the Roman name of which may have been Dasianis – must have been a relatively desirable posting for the troops, probably from the Third Cyrenaica Legion, who manned it. The fort may have been remodelled under Constantine or Jovian (363–4). But much of what can now be seen

Interior of the fort.

represents an energetic reconstruction undertaken in 1237 under the Ayyubid governor, Azzadin Aybak, and proudly recorded in an inscription above the gate on the south-west front. Thereafter little happened until the arrival of Druze refugees from French rule in Syria, who occupied Azraq in the 1920s and put a number of the buildings into service.

The fort is of the familiar Roman plan, a slightly larger variant of Deir al-Kahf, square with projecting corner towers and additional ones on the outer walls, two flanking the former Roman gateway on the south-east, single towers to the north-east and south-west, and a larger principia built out from the north-west wall, beside a postern, the massive basalt door of which is still in place. Aybak's gate exemplifies the Ayyubids' approach to military architecture. The entrance is through the flank of a substantial tower, the gate defended by a machicolated projection and a pair of basalt doors: once within this any assailant had to negotiate a further door on the right to reach the inner gatehouse, which has a fine corbelled ceiling. The room above this was used by Lawrence, who as the author of a notable book about Crusader castles must have felt the irony of occupying a fortress that had been reconstructed by a follower of Saladin. Two Roman inscriptions have been placed just outside the inner door.

Ranges of buildings line the walls. Some of these more or less adhere to the Roman plan, notably the stables placed against the north-east wall. But much is of the Ayyubid period, including of course the elegant small mosque in the centre, its position determined by the need for the mihrab to face Mecca: the corbelled roof rests on two rows of twin arches, supported in the middle by inverted column bases.

About 2 kilometres/1¼ miles from the fort is a second monument of some interest, 'Ain as-Sil, reached by forking right on to the old road to Safawi near a petrol station, and turning right after a further kilometre. The black walls of this Umayyad farming complex have no pretension to beauty. The gate on the east side leads through to a courtyard: in the room at the far right corner there is an impressive basalt press; a bath modest was built against the west wall; and there were two large compounds to the north.

The Romans garrisoned Azraq, and the nearby forts at Aseikhin and Uweinid, to defend Syria. Lawrence made it a base for his advance on Damascus. The place can still face both ways. On my first visit sleep was made impossible by a continuous convoy of lorries on the way from Azraq to Baghdad, as Saddam Hussein prepared for his invasion of Kuwait. Some years later my only fellow guests at the resthouse were a party of cheerful Arabs. Apparently impervious to the December nights, they ate outside round a glowing fire, their falcons on perches near by. More recently it was almost disappointing to have the place to myself.

17. ASEIKHIN

Nothing better illustrates the importance to Rome of controlling the Azraq oasis than the intelligence with which the key fort at Azraq itself was supported by satellite fortlets. The more spectacularly placed of these is incontestably Aseikhin. This crowns a prominent conical basalt hill some 15 kilometres/9½ miles north of Azraq. About 13 kilometres/8 miles from the town on the main road to Safawi, a road to the right is marked to the qasr. This is metalled until about a kilometre and a half from the fort, to which a good track continues, cutting a brown swathe up through the basalt. As one walks, it becomes progressively more obvious why the hill was chosen, for the views to the north and east

Arch in west range, looking across towards the oasis.

over the black desert, and to the south over the oasis, are uninterrupted. Aseikhin, so long as this was adequately garrisoned, guarded the northern and eastern approaches to the oasis.

The fort was not large: it did not need to be. The gate was in the centre of the east wall. The arch within is in place. The door behind opened to a rectangular courtyard, with two doors in the opposite wall, and three on the narrower lateral ones. There is no evidence that any of the ranges was of more than a single storey, but the roofs were borne on arches, one of which, in the central room on the left, remains in place. The arches were of carefully dressed blocks, but otherwise the relentlessly black basalt masonry is of a rather rough quality. No inscriptions have been found to establish the name of this isolated outpost.

The Romans were not the first to see the potential of the hill. For lower down it is girdled with a wall of irregular lumps of basalt. Desert kites, the low walls built to trap wild animals from the Neolithic period onwards, have been recognized near by; and Thamudic inscriptions have been found on boulders in the area. For millennia early man hunted for food and grazed his flocks in this uncompromising terrain.

18. QASR AL-UWEINID

A second outlying fort that supported the Roman base at Azraq was Qasr al-Uweinid, less dramatically placed than Aseikhin but nonetheless in a commanding position. The road south from the modern town passes to the west of the reservoir at Shishan, with basalt walls of early date, which have most recently been attributed to the Umayyad period. After 7 kilometres/4½ miles, take the turn to the right for Shaumari, and then turn right to follow a track towards the basalt ridge on the opposite side of the wide Wadi Butm, which is sometimes grazed by camels.

The fort hugs the western extremity of the lava outcrop some 4 kilometres/2½ miles from the turn. The position was clearly chosen because it commanded the approaches to the oasis from the south-west. The unusual asymmetrical plan was no doubt determined by the site, which was most vulnerable from the level ground to the east, and protected by the steep encircling bank of the wadi to the south and west. The north and south walls run at angles of roughly 100 degrees from this to the east, but are shorter than it: the west wall is stepped back near the centre to accommodate both the gate, part of the left side of which is in place, and a substantial tower, now much tumbled, which is set back within the south angle of the defences. Walls of other buildings, many of which have been illicitly excavated, line the irregular central courtyard. There is a scattering of shards, mostly Roman but some evidently of Islamic date.

Between the gate and the tower was found a fallen lintel with a partly defaced inscription referring to the Emperor Septimius Severus and L. Marius Perpetuus, who was Governor of Arabia between 200 and 202. Another inscription, apparently now removed, records that baths were put up at an unspecified date for the Third Cyrenaica Legion. Uweinid was indeed fortunate, as the Wadi Butm below the site usually flowed in winter. Control of the wadi was secured by a solitary watchtower, black against the encroaching sand, that still stands to a height of some 3.5 metres/12 feet: the visible masonry is of excellent quality. While the fort at Azraq is now hemmed in by the modern town, Qasr al-Uweinid happily still commands an untrammelled landscape. It is not particularly well preserved, and the basalt masonry is more effective than distinguished. Yet towards dusk, as the low light seems to catch every stone and the unyielding black of the basalt is burnished to a deep brown, Uweinid is a place of palpable magic.

19. QASR AL-TUBA

Qasr al-Tuba is the most remote and perhaps the least visited of the Umayyad desert castles of Jordan. It was never finished. But the recently restored ruins are strangely impressive in their isolation. The qasr, built from 743 onwards, was not a princely residence. It was intended to serve as a caravansarai for pilgrims and merchants journeying between the towns of Syria and the lands to the south, who would have taken advantage of the Roman roads further north. The sightseer who wishes to reach Tuba today is less well served. In an ordinary car it is possible to get there from Qasr al-Kharaneh, crossing a wadi some kilometres south of this and then following the track for some 45 kilometres/28 miles until it reaches a metalled road by a group of industrial buildings, the Hazard Waste Disposal. Turn left, and before the road climbs to the east, a sign points to the left. Tuba is about 4 kilometres/2½ miles away, on a track that curves round to the right. An easier approach is from Azraq. Head south and fork right for Ma'an, and 70 kilometres/43½ miles from Azraq, turn right opposite a petrol station, grandly named the Al Tuba Palace Rest Area, on a poorly maintained road and continue for 14 kilometres/8½ miles, until you see the disposal unit on the left: the sign, only marked on the opposite side, is on the right. Don't expect any workman who happens to be about to be of help: just beyond the turn a lorry driver, himself perhaps ill at ease in his loneliness, assured me with evident conviction that Tuba was 100 kilometres/62 miles further on, and it was only after I turned that I saw the sign. In addition there is a good new road, marked to both the qasr and the disposal unit, from a point 22 kilometres/14 miles north of Al-Qatrana on the Desert Highway: this reaches the sign after 47 kilometres/29 miles.

On my first visit I followed the very rough track for a couple of miles, towards a group of bushes that were promising signs in this naked landscape. Abandoning the car, I walked on for a mile or so, for remote buildings should be approached with respect and given the space these deserve. Tuba is on the south-east side of the wide Wadi al-Ghadaf, the ground strewn with flint. The scale of the project matched this setting. The plan was rectangular, aligned from the north-west to the south-east, with two virtually identical sections each some 70 metres/230 feet square, both with entrances to the north-east leading to courtyards which were in turn to be linked by a narrow corridor, set within an outer wall punctuated with semicircular towers, four at either end, seven to the south-west and three with the paired square gatehouse towers to the north-west. The footings are of stone, but the walls above were of fired brick capped by mud brick. Only the north-west section of the complex was completed, and of this only the block at the north corner survives to any height. But even this seems substantial, with its generous barrel-vaulted rooms, roofed in brick. Mud brick is a vulnerable material and much inevitably has been lost. But the relatively recent restoration has been tactful. The eroded wall that runs to the east corner and the

north-west section have not been touched. In the south-east area work was hardly carried above the foundations. Sadly the decorated doorways recorded in the past have disappeared, but an elaborately carved lintel in the museum at Amman survives to give some sense of what has been lost.

Water had to be carefully husbanded. There were wells near by, and a barrage in the wadi is no doubt the successor of an earlier dam. But how realistic was it to plant so vast a complex in so remote a position? Was architectural ambition curbed by the death of a particular caliph, by financial problems or by the inadequacy of the water supply? We don't know. But incomplete and eroded as these are, the ruins of Tuba are unaccountably moving in the emptiness of sand and stone and flint.

Below and left (from the west): Qasr al-Tuba.

20. QASR AL-AMRA

Of the so-called desert castles of the Umayyads it is unquestionably Qasr al-Amra that is most eloquent of the *douceur de vivre* of their court. Hardly a generation after this Bedouin dynasty from the Hejaz had won the Caliphate in 661, it embarked on a series of major architectural projects, both in the capital, Damascus, and elsewhere. Qasr al-Amra, which was rediscovered by the Austrian explorer Alois Musil, is not large. Indeed it looks almost insignificant from the modern road that sweeps past the site. But here, as nowhere else, enough of a decorative scheme realized in or after 711, for the Caliph Khalid Ibn al-Walid (705–15) or one of his associates, survives for us to understand something of the artistic horizons of his time, the expression of which would be irrevocably contracted a

few years later as a result of the decision of Yazid II (720–4) to condemn the representation of the human body.

The building served two distinct functions: it housed an audience chamber and a bath complex. It was evidently an element of a more substantial complex that exploited the limited water resources of the upper basin of the Wadi al-Butm, which curves to the west of the site. The qasr and the hydraulic complex beside it were protected from flash floods by a wall, of which only the foundation survives, and which ran out to a sharp angle above the wadi bank. Like other of the 'desert castles', al-Amra can only have been intended for intermittent use, but its original owner, whether the caliph or a member of his family or court, clearly had the most exacting standards.

The main block is of three barrel-vaulted sections, of which the outer two are apsed on the south. The only door is at the centre on the north, and opens to the audience chamber: the central section runs the length of the building, ending in the so-called throne room, while the lateral bays are shorter, to leave space for the two apsed rooms on either side of the latter, and divided from the central space by wide arches that help to support the vaults. The murals for which the qasr is rightly famed suffered from a millennium of neglect and, despite a responsible programme of restoration in 1972, much of the decoration is not easily legible. Field glasses help.

The Umayyads and their artists stood between two worlds: and the al-Amra murals are fascinating in their fusion of east and west. For Talbot Rice these 'are in the main Hellenistic in character', although he saw 'Sasanian influence as well, most clearly exemplified in the ornamental borders'. By the standard of the most accomplished Roman and Byzantine work, the detail may seem relatively crude. Artistically the most memorable of the murals are the two frieze-like hunting compositions of the east wall, the

Qasr al-Amra.

herd of alarmed deer and the determined pack of salukis as they close in on their prey beautifully observed and compelling in their sense of movement. These murals are complemented by vertical scenes showing animals being despatched on the flanking walls. The hunt is presided over by a bearded man who has been assumed to be the proprietor of the qasr and also appears in both the lateral murals. This hypothetical 'Master of Amra' is also seen in the south wall of the right-hand section of the chamber, beside a reclining woman. At the southern end of the west wall is the historically most revealing element of the decoration. This shows the Emperor of Byzantium, Roderick (the last Gothic King of Spain whose defeat in 711 establishes a *terminus post quem* for the murals), the Emperor Chosroes of Persia, the Negus of Abyssinia and two other rulers. Unexpectedly juxtaposed with this charged political statement is a scene with an all but naked woman rising from a bath, observed by, among others, the ubiquitous bearded man. He appears too in the compartment to the right, watching athletes performing. The vaults also were decorated. The relatively well preserved square compartments with representations of tradesmen in the eastern bay offer a microcosm of the commercial and agricultural activities of the time. A crouching female nude survives in the central vault.

A ruler, presumably the caliph, with attendants is seen on the end wall of the 'throne room', the lateral walls of which are treated in compartments with figures placed in niches with half-lengths at the apexes. The chambers at either side are more crudely decorated with plant motifs: scrolling vines, acanthus and pomegranates. The simple mosaic floors are intact.

A door in the east wall of the audience chamber leads to the first room of the bath complex in the wing to the east. This was apparently the apodyterium (changing room) or frigidarium (cold room), with a low bench on two walls. The murals here and in the next rooms are evidently by a different artist, or team of decorators. The heads in the centre of the barrel vault represent the Three Ages of Man; below are animals and figures in diamond-shaped compartments, while the lunettes at either end, one partly sacrificed to enlarge the window, are uncompromisingly salacious. A door on the left leads to the vaulted tepidarium (warm room) which was originally heated by a hypocaust: the tympanum over the entrance is decorated with three women bathing, while the vault is painted with branches that meet at a central boss. The third room, the caldarium (hot room), is notable for the decoration of the dome, showing the night sky centred on the North Star, with the Great and Little Bears, and other groups of stars and signs of the Zodiac: the circumpolar constellations were incorrectly placed by the artist who, it is thought, worked from a celestial globe.

To the north was a key feature of the site, a well driven 40 metres/130 feet down to the water table. The water was raised by an animal-drawn saqiyah, or wheel house, which has been reconstructed. Some 300 metres/328 yards to the north-west are the trifling remains of a watchtower. Jumbled stones 1 kilometre/0.6 miles to the north are all that survive of a castle with a central courtyard that was presumably the main residence of the estate. A few pistachio trees – teberinths – still survive in the wadi to which they gave their name. This drained south-eastwards, past Uweinid, to the oasis of Azraq.

21. QASR AL-KHARANA

Unlike Qasr al-Amra and others of the 'desert castles', Qasr al-Kharana looks the part. The main road sweeps by to the north and pylons stride beside it. But long before the advent of the lorry, ancient tracks across the desert intersected in the level plain, and it has been argued that the Umayyads built the qasr as an outpost from which to maintain their links with the nomad tribes under their control. When it was constructed is not absolutely clear, most probably in the late seventh century, but a *terminus ante quem* is established by a painted graffito in Kufic above the north door of the main upper floor room on the west side with a specific date in the ninety-second year of the Hejira, 24 November 710.

The building, much of which remarkably still stands to full height, is square in plan, with small rounded towers at the corners and in the centres of the sides – of which that to the south is divided into two sections to accommodate the gate – and is built of rough stone. This was originally faced with mortar, a technique that had been used earlier in Sasanian Iran. The outer walls are pierced with rows of arrow slits at two levels: but just as the towers are solid and therefore of very limited use for defensive purposes, so these, placed too high for convenient access for bowmen from the rooms they ventilate, were essentially decorative. Above the upper row runs a frieze of bricks, placed in a herringbone pattern, which emphasizes the width of the façades. Higher up the walls are punctuated by small windows. As the sun moves, shadows are cast by the towers and within the arrow slits and windows.

In the jambs of the generous doorway are two blocks inscribed in Greek, presumably recycled from a Byzantine outpost near by. Pairs of doors at either side of the corridor beyond open to two large barrel-vaulted spaces running the length of the building, each supported on

Qasr al-Kharana from the south-west.

three piers, which were used as stables. The corridor leads to the central courtyard, which was originally flanked by pillars supporting an upper walkway. Stairways lead off this at near ends of the lateral walls; and the three large rooms on the ground floor are reached from the doors at the further ends of these and in the centre of the north wall. Austere, with decoration restricted to a zigzag motif in the plaster, and inevitably dark, these chambers are flanked by sixteen smaller rooms, four of which are linked by the remaining doors from the courtyard.

The staircases lead to the upper floor. This corresponds in plan with that below, except in the south range, where a room is placed above the entrance corridor and a large chamber linked to four small ones above each of the stables. The barrel vaults were constructed of thin stone blocks set in mortar and supported on arches. In the larger chambers these rest on trios of engaged columns; engaged columns are also used, in pairs or groups of three, to flank windows. In some of the larger rooms there are shallow semi-domes, placed on squinches. Most remarkably much of the original plaster survives, testifying to the exacting specifications to which it was made. Moving through the rooms on the south side one realizes that the subtle distinctions between the larger rooms were deliberate: the smaller barrel-vaulted rooms are more or less identical in treatment, with the exception of one next to the westernmost of the larger chambers which has a square ceiling with four subsidiary compartments. Decoration is sparingly used on the arches and in the squinches in the rooms on the south: in those on the west side, which may have been finished marginally later, there are friezes with roundels of stylized plant motifs. The effect is disciplined, but not monotonous. The stairs continue to the roof, the view southwards from which can have changed relatively little since early times until the recent erection of the inevitable visitor centre. A track heads southwards to the desert, to Qasr al-Tuba and to the Nabataean or Roman dam at Jilat. Those who played at the several gameboards scratched into the floors of the qasr must have been keenly aware that it looked out over a landscape they might control but could not hope to tame.

22. QASR AL-MUSHATTA

Time has not been kind to the largest of all the Umayyad 'desert castles', Qasr al-Mushatta, the 'winter palace'. The complex was never finished, whether as a result of changing political circumstances or because of its intended scale; virtually all the decorative carving of the south wall that had survived was taken to Berlin, as a result of Sultan Abdul Hamid II's need to propitiate Kaiser Wilhelm II of Germany, whose government furthered the construction of the Hejaz Railway that passed near by; and the truncated, yet still impressive, ruins are now uncomfortably close to the Queen Alia Airport. Al-Mushatta was first studied by Canon Tristram in 1872, during the groundbreaking expedition recorded in his *Land of Moab*: 'We were astonished', he wrote, 'at the unexpected magnificence of the ruins, unknown to history, and unnamed on the maps.' He believed the qasr to be Sasanian, a view accepted by the Revd William Thompson and by Gertrude Bell: and it was only in the early twentieth century that it was recognized as one of the supreme achievements of Omayyad architecture.

The easiest way to reach the qasr is from the desert highway. Take the turn north of that for the airport, signed to the Jordan Traffic Institute, and follow the subsidiary road south for 2 kilometres/1¼ miles before turning left, passing industrial complexes and crossing the Hejaz Railway: the qasr looms on the left after 7 kilometres/4½ miles, just before a checkpoint.

The Caliph Walid II, who reigned for less than a year in 743–4, is thought to have willed the castle into existence. And the calibre and size of the complex indicate that its builder could count on the concerted resources of the Umayyad state. A square of some 145 metres/475 feet was surrounded by a substantial wall, 1.7 metres/5½ feet thick, which survives in places to a height of 5.5 metres/18 feet, with substantial rounded corner towers and five smaller semicircular towers on each side, except that on the south, where there are four and the central gate is flanked by two towers. The lower few courses of the wall were of finely cut masonry, but above fired brick was used. To the right of the gate is a section of the carved decoration that the Germans were considerate enough to leave. But it takes a degree of imagination to visualize the intended impact of the building. Above a decorated base there was a wide band carved with a continuous row of projecting chevrons, in the interstices between which, set in fields of plant motifs, were richly carved hexafoils; the whole was surmounted by a cornice. Coptic and Sasanian influences have been detected in the detail, and distinctions in detail between the sections from either side of the door may reflect the employment of rival groups of masons: Lankester Harding comments on 'the rather indifferent quality' of their work, which was carved *in situ*. The blocks that survive on the site show that his verdict was unduly harsh.

Within the walls, the qasr was laid out in three sections, the widest in the centre. The projected buildings in the lateral sections were never begun, but some evidence of their intended disposition is offered by the stones that project from the outer walls, which would have been bonded with the masonry of the internal buildings. In the first part of the central section there were to have been balancing ranges, including a mosque, of which the foundations survive. Beyond these was a large open courtyard. Ahead is the palace proper. The great expanse of unrelieved brick is pierced by the triple entrance, which is on the pattern of a Roman triumphal arch, with a large central opening flanked by smaller ones. The surviving original blocks of the latter have been put back, with new ones substituted for those that have been lost; and in December 2010 the centrings were in place for the central arch. The three doors led to a great aisled hall, two of the lateral columns of which have been re-erected. This opens to the tri-apsidal throne room. Some of the carved voussoirs of the hall lie where these fell, but the brick vaults have gone.

Fallen voussoirs.

Doors off the hall led to matching courts from which the rooms of the flanking ranges were reached. The barrel vaults of two of these are intact and others survive in part: these were built of burnt bricks, rather than the dried ones employed at Qasr al-Tuba, the design of which in some respects parallels that at Mushatta.

Canon Tristram saw herds of gazelle in the area. And an abundance of game might explain why Walid II, who was known for his love of hunting, chose to build so lavish a residence on the desert fringe. Equally the brevity of his caliphate would offer a plausible reason for the fact that the qasr and its remarkable decoration were never finished. Alternatively work may have continued under Walid's successor, Marwan II, whose reign came to an abrupt end with the Abbasid victory of 750. When the wind is from the desert, we can still ignore the warehouses to the west and sense something of the Umayyads' taste for the open spaces their ancestors had known.

23. AL-QASTAL

Some places excite us because they are difficult to reach; others only deserve to be visited because we have to pass them. The latter is the case with Qastal, some 6 kilometres/3¾ miles west of Mushatta, just across the Desert Highway. Thought to have been a Roman fort by Canon Tristram and other early travellers, including Gertrude Bell, whose descriptions show how much the site has suffered in the interim, Qastal was rather an Umayyad foundation, although it was subsequently used under the Ayyubids and during the Mameluke ascendancy. It crowns a low tell, with commanding views in every direction, which explains why part of the qasr has now been claimed for a monitoring post.

The square plan, like that of other Omayyad complexes, was no doubt strongly influenced by Roman forts. Some 68 metres/223 feet square, Qastal thus enclosed an area approximately half the size of Qasr al-Tuba and a quarter of that of Mushatta. Here also there were large rounded towers at the corners and smaller subsidiary semicircular ones between them, three on each side except to the east where there were four, two of which flanked the main entrance. Within the walls were six bayts, or blocks, each with four rooms off an open court, ranged round the central courtyard. The extant walls are of fine dressed masonry, and although nothing survives above the level of the first floor, there are thought to have been two storeys. The eastern section is the best preserved, although a later extension has been built out from the northern part of it. The left jamb and the fallen lintel, both decorated, of the east gate survive. Simple mosaics in some of the rooms of the south range are intact. And at the south-west corner of the paved central courtyard a stair under a beautiful shell niche descends to a cistern that has now been largely filled in.

Detail of the east gate.

Immediately to the north, and evidently contemporary with the qasr, is the mosque, which is entered from the opposite side, through a court of which the west wall is partly intact. The mosque itself may originally have been roofed in wood, but was covered with a barrel vault at a relatively early date. The prayer hall, 5 metres/16 feet deep and 16 metres/52 feet wide with a central mihrab and two small windows at either end, seemed 'immense' to Miss Bell, who assumed that it was part of a Roman fortlet, and it is indeed strangely impressive in its austere simplicity. The round tower at the north-west corner, now alas with rather less of the decoration — 'rinceaux above and fluted triglyphs below, with narrow blank metopes between them' — she described, which still stands to a height of 6 metres/20 feet, is one of the earliest extant minarets. To the west was an early Islamic cemetery, inscribed stones from which are now in the museum at Madaba. The complex was served by a substantial cistern, 1 kilometre/0.6 miles to the north-west, and by a dam to the east. For the sounds of traffic on the Desert Highway and the proximity of modern buildings should not make us forget the infrastructure that made it possible for the Umayyads to maintain so palatial an establishment on the margin of the desert.

24. THE KING'S HIGHWAY

Ancient roads have a strong hold upon the imagination. Brought up as I was in a village touched by a Roman road only a few miles from that great thoroughfare of early Britain, the Ridgeway, I have always sensed their appeal. The somewhat portentously named King's Highway, which runs southwards from Philadelphia (Amman), also follows a ridge, the line of the hills to the east of the Dead Sea and the valley to the south of this, the Wadi Araba. This road through the lands of the ancient kingdoms of Ammon, Moab and Edom was already ancient when it was mentioned in the Book of Numbers (chapter 20, 14–21): as Tyndale and later translators of the Bible recognized, the Hebrew word used had no royal connotations. Moses sent messengers to the King of Edom, asking for passage through his territory:

> We will go by the highway and neither turn unto the right hand
> nor to the left, until we be past thy country.

The king was rash enough to refuse. Half a millennium later the highway was maintained by the Nabataeans, and carried the commodities – spices from India that had been shipped to the port of Qana on the Yemeni coast and the yet more prized frankincense of Arabia Felix – to the trade in which their kingdom owned its wealth.

As a result of Trajan's forward policy in the east, the road was upgraded to serve the Roman military machine, facilitating troop movements and communications between the forts that guarded the desert frontier. The Via Nova Traiana remained the main artery of the land under Byzantine, Muslim and Crusader rule, and was only superseded under the Ottomans in the sixteenth century, when a shorter alternative route, the Tariq al-Bint, the predecessor of the modern Desert Highway, was favoured for pilgrims on the Haj to Mecca.

A series of historic towns lay on the King's Highway: Hesban, where the dusty tell has yielded evidence of successive occupation from early times: Madaba, Dhiban, Rabba and Karak, among others. The road traverses spectacular country, not least when it crosses the deep valleys of the Wadi Mujib, the ancient Arnon, and the Wadi Hasa, the brook Zered of the Bible. Inevitably the line has been altered to suit modern modes of transport, most obviously where the road crosses the two great wadis: as a result a considerable stretch of the Roman paved road can be followed beyond the Wadi Hasa, where its successor takes a route some way to the west. The historic role of the King's Highway as the spinal cord of the country between the Rift Valley and the desert will quickly seem evident to the observant sightseer. And although most of the ancient sites that cluster round the road are, with the exception of Karak, very much less spectacular than Jerash or Petra, these cumulatively offer a remarkable microcosm of the way successive civilizations have impinged on the area.

Hesban: the tell.

25. MADABA

Madaba is justly famed for one mosaic, but there is much more to the town than a map, however remarkable. There would be even more if some ninety Christian families had not moved in 1879 from Kerak and occupied the long-abandoned tell of what had originally been a Moabite town. Taken by the Israelites, who then assigned it to the tribe of Reuben, this was recovered, to the dismay of the Prophet Isaiah, for Moab in the ninth century BC, by King Mesha, as is proudly stated on that monarch's stela found at Dhiban and now in the Louvre. In the second century BC Madaba was held by the Nabataeans, from whom it was taken by the Jewish John Hyrcanus in about 110 BC. Hyrcanus II ceded the city to the Nabataean king, Aretas III, in return for help in recovering Jerusalem from his own brother, and this remained under Nabatean control until the kingdom passed to Rome in AD 106. Incorporated in the province of Asia, Madaba became a base of the Third Cyrenaica Legion and a significant walled town, with the elegant amenities that prolonged prosperity made possible: column-lined main streets, temples and other public buildings.

Christianity had taken root by the time of Diocletian (284–305) when Madaba lost her quota of martyrs, the names of no fewer than eight of whom are recorded. Their cult was no doubt remembered in the ensuing century when Christianity became the official religion. An episcopal see by 451, Madaba flourished in the following century, notably under the Emperor Justinian (527–65); and it is to this period that most of the major extant mosaics belong. The Christian presence remained strong in the Umayyad period, and Madaba was the seat of a bishop until at least 785. The place was not abandoned until the Mameluke period.

Modern Madaba sprawls far beyond the spreading tell of its predecessors. There are still Christian communities, but these are now very much in the minority. Near the centre of the town, just east of Talal Street which intersects this, is the unprepossessing Greek Orthodox Church of St George, built in 1896. Because the Ottoman government permitted the erection of churches only on the sites of earlier ones, this was superimposed on the foundations of a Byzantine building, parts of the sixth-century mosaic floor of which had been identified by a priest a few years earlier. Only a quarter of the mosaic survived, but this was preserved as part of the floor of the new structure.

The complete mosaic measured 15.6 metres/51 feet by 6 metres/20 feet, and constituted a map of the area from Sidon and Tyre in what is now the Lebanon in the north to the delta of the Nile in the south and from the Mediterranean to the eastern deserts. The map is orientated, and the towns are depicted in perspective. In the principal extant section of very irregular shape the Jordan, with its complement of outsize fish, flows from the left into the Dead Sea, on which two boats ply; to the east are mountain ridges rising to the south, while the Lissan is shown with palm trees; at the upper tip, at the head of a straightened valley, is Kerak, identified as [Chara]chmoba – the delta is on the extreme right; and near the centre at the bottom the ports of Ashdod, Askalon and Gaza can be made out. Happily an area of loss largely misses the representation of Jerusalem, girt within its walls, with its colonnaded street and, just below this, the Church of the Holy Sepulchre. To the right of Jerusalem is Bethlehem, and to the left, by the tip of the lost section, Jericho. Inscriptions lie thickly across the more densely inhabited areas of Palestine, many naming places with religious connotations. The Madaba map is not a great work of art, but with their controlled use of brown and reddish and paler tesserae the craftsmen who worked on it created a remarkable historic document.

Behind the church, on Hussein Bin Ali Street, is the so-called Burnt Palace. This was built in the sixth century and burnt in the eighth, and is most interesting for its mosaics: the animal scenes have a certain vigour,

Mukhayyat: mosaic.

while the representation of Tyche, so popular under imperial Rome, seems something of a throwback. Continue in the same direction for the Archeological Park, near the entrance to which is an early decorative mosaic of Hellenistic character from Herod's fortress-palace of Machaerus. Further on, a raised walkway crosses a section of Roman road to buildings respectively of 607–9 and 595–6, and then crosses this again to the so-called Hippolytus Hall, a grand room in a sixth-century mansion which was buried when the Church of the Virgin was constructed.

The room takes its name from a mosaic of Phaedra and Hippolytus. Behind this is a scene with Venus and Adonis, the former chastising Cupid, and the Graces. The border is decorated with hunting scenes, always appealing to patrician taste, beyond which, implying the sense of place of the patron, are women representing Rome, Gregoria and Madaba itself. The walkway continues to above the nave of the Church of the Virgin, with an elaborate geometrical mosaic of 767, which replaced the late

Mukhayyat: mosaic.

sixth-century original, some flowers from which can still be made out. The designer was constrained by the strictly applied rules of Iconoclasm. But he clearly shared the preoccupation of contemporary architects with reconciling circular and square forms: here the central roundel is set within two overlapping squares, placed diagonally, the extremities of which are placed within an outer circle. Further on there is a courtyard with further mosaics from Ma'in, including representations of Hesban and Gadaron, now Salt, which remind us that the celebrated map was not conceived in isolation. A mosaic of an ox was carefully censored in the eighth century when Iconoclasm was so rigorously enforced by the Eastern Church.

One of the most distinguished mosaics at Madaba is in the Church of the Apostles, some 400 metres/437 yards to the south off Nuzlia Street. The church, of basilica plan, was of 578. The central medallion of the mosaic in the nave represents the sea, with a partly naked woman, clearly inspired by earlier representations of Thetis, emerging from the waves, attended by a court of fish and marine monsters. Around this is an inscription referring to Anastasius, Thomas and Theodora, which most remarkably gives the name of the mosaicist, Salaman. The rest of the field is decorated with paired birds in confrontation, their wings used with plant forms to frame diagonal compartments, while the acanthus border is enriched with animals and a scene of a boy drawn by two birds. There are three further mosaics in chapels north of the nave: the central one is of a type that was evidently popular, with four trees rising from the corners, their tops meeting at a central circle, with animals grazing peacefully below. The most perfect example of the design is in the Church of Saints Lot and Procopius at Mukhayyat, the ancient Nebo, some 16 kilometres/10 miles north-west of Madaba, off the road to the spectacularly sited but ruthlessly commercialized church of Mount Nebo.

The Madaba Museum is some minutes' walk to the west of the Church of the Apostles. This incorporates a number of houses built after Madaba was reoccupied, in an area that the Byzantines had also used for residential purposes. The mosaics are of some interest. There is one of a damaged Bacchic procession, and a small but complete floor with the Lamb grazing in front of a tree in a domestic chapel, which was subsequently incorporated in the Misaad al-Twal house. The other finds are of more limited appeal.

26. MACHAERUS: MUKAWIR

There are few places where the past can be so clearly read as at the fortress-palace of Machaerus, high in the chain of hills that hang over the eastern shore of the Dead Sea. The steep ridge on which it stood is cut off from higher ground to the south-east and rises between deep valleys, dominating lower ridges to the north that flank the Wadi Zarka as it sinks towards the inland sea. The place came to prominence as a result of the rebellion of the Maccabees against the Seleucids, and the Hasmonaean Alexander Jannaeus (103–76 BC) fortified Machaerus, as he did the now more celebrated site at Masada across the Dead Sea. He was succeeded by his widow, Salome Alexandra; but subsequently strife between their elder son Hyrcanus (not to be confused with his Tobiad namesake, the builder of Iraq al-Amir) and his brother Aristobulus led to Pompey's capture of Jerusalem from the latter in 63 BC. Aristobulus's son, Alexander, held Machaerus, but was in turn attacked by the Romans, who were assisted by Antipater, an Idumean adventurer. Machaerus fell in 56 BC, and the luckless Aristobulus was borne off to Rome. In his place, the Romans nominated as king Antipater's son, Herod the Great, who strengthened his claims by marriage to a member of the Hasmonaean family. Herod built a substantial palace within the fortress, no doubt using it as a base for visits to his thermal complex of Kallirhoe in the Zarka Valley. On Herod's death in 4 BC his sons split their inheritance, Galilee and Peraea – the land between the Zarka and the Arnon – falling to Herod Antipas. He held Machaerus, and, as Josephus records, it was here that Salome demanded the head of St John the Baptist, whose message would in any case have sounded deeply disconcerting to anyone in Herod's position. A Jordanian guide I overheard at Ajlun summarized the outcome to perfection: 'He killed John Baptist after party.'

We can only speculate as to where Salome danced before Herod and received delivery of the Baptist's head. Josephus' history means that we have a much clearer knowledge of the eventual fate of Machaerus itself. Although manned by a Roman garrison at the outbreak of the Jewish Revolt of AD 66, the fortress was seized by rebels. Six years later the Romans finally closed in. Their general, Lucilius Bassus, clearly understood that he could leave nothing to chance. Machaerus was invested with a ruthless efficiency, as the remains of siege walls and camps demonstrate. The zealots must have felt increasingly exposed as they were cut off from the hinterland by a line of circumvallation and then watched impotently from above as the Roman engineers gained inexorably on their defences. Demoralized further by the loss of one of their leaders, Eleazar, they surrendered, possibly even before the siege works were completed. Machaerus was sacked, as was the town that had grown up below it on the north-east flank of the ridge. The town was apparently a place of pilgrimage in the Byzantine era, but when in 1872 Canon Tristram attained his 'long-cherished day-dream' of exploring it he found no ruin worthy of being photographed.

A road from the successor village, Mukawir, descends towards the saddle that divides the ridge crowned by the fortress from the higher ground. The aqueduct that crossed this can be traced. Higher up there are some small caves. The top of the hill was protected by an outer wall with substantial towers of Hasmonaean date on the south-west side and at the exposed north-west salient. The Herodian baths were just east of the former, while Herod's palace – which was evidently a complex of considerable sophistication – was built over the original fortress. The Romans tore it down, and the re-erected columns can only hint at what has gone. What takes the breath away is the plunging view down to the Dead Sea and across to the hills of Palestine.

Roman siege wall in morning light.

Machaerus is particularly rewarding in the evening and the early morning. The low light catches the remains of the siege works: the great ramp that was rising towards the north-west tower when the zealots surrendered, and the 3 kilometres/2 miles of siege walls that cross the lateral valleys and crest the opposite ridges, with strategically placed fortlets. By the time I had followed the Roman walls to the west, the thought of motoring on in the half-light to Kerak palled. I decided to trust to the unyielding floor, confident that the sheepdogs guarding the flocks in the valleys would warn me of any untoward movement. The crescent of the new moon and stars beyond number hung as a canopy above the columns, and soon I ceased to care that of the nearest of these, only the capital was real. There was no more appropriate place to spend Christmas Eve, for the distant aura of the lights of Jerusalem was in sight beyond the Dead Sea. It was cold, but modern sleeping bags are warm. And my reward when I woke and moved to the wall above the ramp was to watch as the light stole round, touching first the columns and then the flanks of the higher ridges, before igniting the line of the siege walls below. The dramatic cliffs and deep canyons beyond the Dead Sea in turn began to glow. After attacking a packet of Bath Olivers, I set off to follow the Roman walls. As I made up the ridge to the west, a flock of sheep came down towards me, luminous in the low sunlight. The herdsman was puzzled by my presence.

27. UMM AL-WALID and AL-QANATIR

Umm al-Walid ('mother of children'), approximately 13 kilometres/8 miles east of Madaba, has a long history of occupation. On the approach from the west, to the left of the road and below this, is a small Roman fort or way station, which may have been abandoned in the fifth century, hardly worth detailed examination. In the centre of the town is a more impressive, if smaller, structure of excellent bossed masonry, a temple which was incorporated in an Umayyad complex: a donkey is tethered in the ruinous forecourt and children play. Much more impressive, although only the lower elements of the walls are in place, is the Umayyad qasr on the eastern fringe of the village.

The site was evidently chosen for its commanding view eastwards to the desert. The plan is characteristic, laid out on a square with rounded towers at the corners and on the walls. The gate to the east is set within a larger rounded tower, and decorated with small twin pilasters at either side. This led into a large courtyard, the original paving of which is largely intact. The bases of a screen of columns survive on the entrance side. Ranges of buildings lined the walls, and there was a mosque.

Despite the unselfconscious charm of the place, it might not merit a detour but for the two splendid dams, also of the Umayyad period and evidently associated in some way with the complex, which lie 2 kilometres/1¼ miles to the east, near the village of Al-Qanatir. The road that skirts the qasr runs downhill to a deep valley and then descends to a further wadi. One of the dams is immediately in view to the left of the road as it climbs up towards a low ridge. This is the east dam. The south side has apparently been replaced with regular courses of smallish blocks, each successive row recessed slightly. The masonry on the north by contrast is very similar to that of parts of the wall of the qasr, with courses of very much larger blocks, divided horizontally by lines of much thinner stones: the core of the dam was of cement. Two run-offs for water can be seen. At the west end there seems to have been a leet. The dam was not maintained by the Umayyads' successors, and as a result the ground to the west was eroded by flash floods.

The west dam is rather more than a kilometre/0.6 miles from the road, and less easily seen from this. Turn back towards Umm al-Walid and look down the wadi to the north, which is now on your right. A track leads to an abandoned building on the ridge to the west of the dam. The west dam, to which water was originally channelled from its counterpart, is substantially the longer of the two. But it loses much in impact, because it has been coated in concrete and unsympathetically repointed. This restoration may have contributed to a relatively recent breach in the centre, which has, however, the merit of revealing the original cemented rubble core. There are two run-off drains in the western section, and at the east end is a reasonably well preserved leet, which was used for a mill.

The two dams serve to remind us that the Umayyads could only indulge their taste for planting great establishments in the desert fringe, and sustain great agricultural projects of the kind that they achieved at Resafe and Qasr el-Heir in Syria, if they exploited every possible means of water collection. In building major dams they were following the example of their predecessors, the Romans and the Nabataeans, whose dam in the Wadi Jilat between the Desert Highway and Qasr al-Tuba is equally ambitious in scale, and indeed the Hittites, who dammed the upper waters of the Orontes to create Lake Qattina.

Al-Qanatir: the west dam.

28. UMM AR-RASAS

Umm ar-Rasas has been transformed in recent decades. On my first visit there was little to see except the large Roman fort, its walls strengthened by projecting towers. The area within was literally choked with fallen masonry, among which the pattern of walls could be traced, and from which the occasional low arch projected. Masons were at work, protected by their keffiyehs (headdresses) from the spring sun. Now the sightseer can gain a far fuller understanding of what was a major settlement on the plain of Moab, mentioned in the Bible as Mephaath. The scale of the site offers telling evidence of agricultural prosperity. The Nabataeans posted a *strategos* – or regional governor – here; while the Romans clearly stationed a considerable garrison at their Mefaat to defend the desert frontier, as the ecclesiastical historian Eusebius implied in 293.

A hundred or so years later we learn from the Notitia Dignitatum that the 'elite native cavalry' was based at Mefa, which as the number of its churches implies continued to flourish in the Byzantine era. Men of the town killed an early follower of Muhammed, Zayd ibn 'Amr Nuqil but, as the splendid eighth-century mosaics found at Umm ar-Rasas prove, Christianity continued to flourish there well into the Abbasid period.

On reaching the modern village take a road on the left, which doubles back towards an unusually tall and narrow tower. This is decorated with a niche to the east and crosses on the other sides. The tower is solid but at the top there is a narrow chamber with windows. The corners of the upper stage, above a run-off to deflect water, are marked by pilasters, bonded into the masonry, with elaborately carved capitals, now much eroded. It has been claimed that the tower was intended for a stylite, and although this is very different in character from known stylite columns and the early representation of one at Deir Mar Mousa in Syria, there is no other plausible explanation: the tower clearly had a religious significance, as it is shown prominently in a mosaic in the Church of St Stephen. Some confused echo of its origin is implied by the name, the Tower of the Christian Lady, recorded by Canon Tristram, who camped at Umm ar-Rasas for a week in 1872. Below the tower there is a small church. A little to the north is a second, more conventional tower, and beyond this a rock-cut cistern and a small quarry.

The main settlement south of the village, now entered through a visitor centre even bigger than that of the citadel at Amman, is dominated by the hangar protecting the mosaics, which lies to the north of the rectangular fort. But it makes sense to examine the latter first. There were three gates, the most elaborate on the east, the others in the longer south and north walls, the last not centrally placed, presumably because the area outside it had already been developed when the fortress was laid out.

The south wall of the Roman fort.

Eventually all but the north gate were blocked. There were four churches in the fort. Two, side by side against the east wall, are of the sixth century: fragmentary mosaics are in place, that on the left with scrolling acanthus fronds. These have been cleared, but otherwise the fort still looks very much as it did in Tristram's time.

Leaving by the north gate you reach the civilian settlement, in which no fewer than eleven churches have been found. This was not laid out on a formal plan. Moving towards the hangar, you pass the church that takes its name from a mosaic with two lions. Further north is a cluster of four churches of varying date. The mosaics of two of these well deserve the protection they have been given. The northernmost of the four churches was founded by Bishop Sergius in 586, as the dedicatory inscription in the mosaic of the raised presbytery establishes. This is decorated with rams and fruiting pomegranate trees. Sadly the large mosaic of the nave with portraits of donors and representations of the earth and the sea suffered grievously at the hands of Iconoclasts, who failed to destroy a personification of one of the seasons at the top right corner only because it had been covered by a pulpit.

The adjacent Church of St Stephen lies immediately to the south. Here the dedicatory inscription in the presbytery mosaic, which is decorated with interlacing geometrical patterns, establishes a date of 785. The clou of the site is unquestionably the great mosaic of the nave. The central field is decorated with a vine, rising in four rows of eleven circular tendrils. Borders with boats, marine creatures representing the Nile and ten named places situated on the delta surround it. Flanking these at either side are bands that ran under the lateral arcades, with depictions of towns, all of which are identified. On the right the sequence begins from the eastern end with a double panel showing 'Kastron Mefaa': above is a gate flanked by towers with windows at three levels and below this a reasonably accurate depiction of the stylite tower, shown in an enclosure behind an arcaded structure. Beneath this Philadelphia

(Amman), Madaba, Esbounta (Hesban), Belemounta (Ma'in), Areopolis (Rabba) and Charachmoba (Karak) are shown, all as walled towns with towers of similar type. Opposite, headed appropriately by Jerusalem, are seven other towns of Palestine, Nablus, Sebastis, Ceasarea, Diospolis, Eleutheropolis, Askalon and Gaza: the buildings in these are described less uniformly than those of their counterparts, Nablus with a no doubt reused pedimented classical temple, Sebastis with an arcade in two tiers, Askalon with an octagonal shrine. In the aisles there are wider fields: that on the right with alternating round and square compartments, each with a plant or fruit motif; its counterpart with an interlacing pattern framing pairs of square panels with still lifes. Above these are buildings symbolizing two further local towns, that on the right Diblaton, perhaps Dhiban, beside a well-pruned but inevitably stylized pear tree with four heavy fruits, while its counterpart to the left, Limbon, which has been tentatively identified as Libb, is flanked by a pomegranate. The patrons of the church, whose names are so proudly paraded in this, little knew that the pavement to which they contributed would represent a final high point in a long-established local artistic tradition.

29. LEHUN

It would be an exaggeration to claim that the discoveries made by the Belgian excavators at Lehun are among the more impressive monuments of ancient Jordan. But the site, astride a valley that hangs over the prodigious canyon of the Wadi Mujib, is memorable, and for the sightseer bound from Umm er-Rasas to the King's Highway at Dhiban, a detour of no more than 4 kilometres/2½ miles is necessary.

In few places is the evidence of as many phases of occupation so readily seen, in part because of the excellence of the archaeologists' signs. On the approach is a road to the right signed to the castle. This crosses to the west flank of the valley and ends at a small car park. Beyond are the partly excavated footings of a substantial fortified village, datable between 1300 and 1000 BC, and thus to the Late Bronze and Early Iron Age, when the kingdom of Moab is first mentioned in Egyptian sources. Twenty out of a total of between sixty and a hundred houses, each occupied by as many as ten people, have been examined. In about 900 BC (Iron Age II), a Moabitic fortress was built between the village and the top of the ravine, no doubt to monitor movement in the valley below. The fort was shaped like a somewhat distorted square, with corner towers extending within rather than outside the line of the walls, as was subsequently to become customary.

The town lay to the east. On the west side of the wadi are the foundations of a Roman temple, Ayyubid buildings and a mosque of the Mameluke period, as well as small caves that were in use in Ottoman times. Opposite is the cella of a small partly reconstructed Nabataean temple, of beautifully controlled bossed masonry. A little higher up, nearer the houses of the living village, are other buildings, as yet unexcavated, and cisterns. The site museum to the south is not always open.

30. AL QASR and RABBA

South of the Wadi Mujib, the King's Highway crosses the prosperous plateau of Moab. A number of sites are in reach, and the motorist should at least pause to see what survives in two of the ancient towns on the road.

The first is Al Qasr. Near the centre of the modern settlement, among unprepossessing concrete buildings to the left of the road, are the ruins of a distinguished Nabataean temple, known as the Beit al-Karm. Enough remains for it to be relatively easy to imagine what has gone. The outer walls are of up to fourteen courses of beautifully graded masonry. Movement was given to the side and rear elevations, as can still be seen on the north, by stepping back the central sections of the walls above the second exposed course, so that the corner sections stand forwards. The temple was entered through a recessed portico, with four

Al Qasr: portico of the Nabatean temple.

outsize columns, of which the bases are in place, and three doors. An antechamber leads to the cella, which was in three sections.

Steps in the south-west of these led to an upper floor, of which nothing now remains. A litter of carved blocks, including a fine Corinthian capital and sections of acanthus decoration, shows that this was a building of considerable elegance, of a type most familiar from its very much more ambitious counterpart at Petra. Within the fence protecting the site there is a cistern, one section of the arched roof of which remains in place. The juxtaposition of the two structures is not accidental, for water catchment and storage were of vital importance to the Nabataeans.

Five kilometres/3 miles further on is Rabba, the Rabbath Moab of the Old Testament, which as Areopolis was a significant post on the Via Nova Traiana. Columns have been re-erected by the main road. On the right is the somewhat untidy archaeological site. The most memorable building is the Roman temple, its portal flanked by two generous niches framed by pilasters, of which only that to the right is complete, its Corinthian capital now at a precarious angle. The niches originally framed statues of the co-Emperors Diocletian and Maximian, to whom the temple was dedicated. They reigned together from 286 to 305, and Diocletian took a close interest in the defence of Syria, giving his name to the ungraded northern counterpart of the Via Nova Traiana, the Strata Diocletiana, that ran from Sura on the Euphrates by way of Palmyra to Damascus. We know the name of the cavalry who were stationed at Areopolis, the Equites Mauri Illyriciani. The cella of the temple had been much altered and the arches within this, one springing from a fine Corinthian capital, are later interpolations. Near the temple is part of a road, in which basalt blocks contrast with pale slabs of limestone. To the south-west are three cisterns, two of considerable size, their scale eloquent of the needs of the substantial Roman town.

31. LEJJUN

East of the King's Highway, midway between Karak, where the route up from the southern end of the Dead Sea reached this, and the margin of the desert, is the formidable legionary fortress of the Romans at Lejjun. The site was intelligently chosen, for the Wadi al-Lejjun is fed by a perennial spring. The fortress was apparently built in about AD 300 as part of Diocletian's programme to defend the frontier, the Limes Arabicus, from the desert tribes over which imperial Rome could exercise no effective control. The march was garrisoned by the locally raised Legio IV Martia, and the fortress seems to have been the Betthorus of the Notitia Dignitatum. Originally it housed some two thousand soldiers, but perhaps as the result of an earthquake in 363, this complement subsequently halved. The importance of the fortress diminished further in the Byzantine era, partly because the Emperor Justinian had higher priorities; and Lejjun was abandoned after a further earthquake in 551. Over a millennium and a half later the Ottomans, whose imperial power in turn was under threat, built two rows of barrack blocks on higher ground a few hundred metres to the west, for similar strategic and practical reasons.

The rectangular fortress was laid out on more or less gently sloping ground south of the wadi. Although much stone was removed by the Ottomans to build their barracks, enough survives for one to gain a clear idea of the plan: there were rounded corner towers and smaller rounded towers between them, six on the longer north and south sides, and four to the east and west, the central pairs flanking the four gateways. Nothing survives to full height. But the scale of the fort is impressive, and there is something rather moving about the skeletal arch that still somehow holds its own amid the mass of fallen masonry. The best-preserved of the corner towers is that at the north-west. The excavated north gate led

Arch in the walls.

to the via principalis, at the junction of which with the via praetoria from the east there was a monumental gate, the groma. To the west of this was a space before the principia, which as its purpose dictated was the most substantial building within the fortress. The garrison was originally accommodated in eight barrack ranges, each of eighteen pairs of rooms: after 363 these were modified. A late alteration was the provision of a small church within the north wall, behind the range on the west side of the via principalis. The remains are vestigial.

The east wall in particular has suffered from erosion. For ruins, particularly those which have been excavated and not covered, are vulnerable, as I saw only too clearly on my first visit in heavy rain, which reminded me of childhood visits to Hadrianic forts in Northumberland. Little of interest to the amateur is to be seen of the vicus that grew up round the fortress, and like this was, except in the winter, largely dependent on water channelled from a dam below the spring to the west. Diocletian's engineers clearly took the view that the proximity of water outweighed the fact that the site was overlooked by higher ground. But this meant that Betthorus was vulnerable to surprise attack, despite the proximity to the north-east of Qasr Bshir (no. 32). This may explain its signalling posts. The Romans took over an Iron Age fort high on the scarp on the further side of the wadi, above the point where this turns sharply to the south, the Khirbet al-Fityan. The north gate has been partly excavated, and there is evidence of barracks and cisterns within: the southern wall and corner towers have partly fallen over the edge of the steep escarpment. The place was clearly chosen for the views it commands, and it is for these that it is most rewarding. Beyond Lejjun can be seen the equally well-positioned tower, Rujm Beni Yasser, from which movements to the east could be monitored.

32. QASR BSHIR

If the visitor to Jordan wishes to see only one Roman fort, the choice is easily made. For Qasr Bshir is not only the best-preserved structure of the type in the Near East, but also perhaps unique in surveying a vast sweep of landscape, sandy and bare, in which three ancient watchtowers are the only other buildings in sight. The place is not on the tourist trail: Lankester Harding, who omitted little, does not so much as mention Bshir; the brief sentence in the *Blue Guide* (1996) admittedly states that it is beautiful; yet but for Kennedy and Riley's illustrations and map reference I might perhaps not have troubled to go. Nothing is known of the history of the place. But we do know its name: the inscription on the lintel above the main gate establishes that the fort was built between 293 and 305:

> To our Best and Greatest Rulers, Gaius Aurelius Valerius Diocletian, Pious,
>   Fortunate, Unconquered Augustus, and Marcus Aurelius Valerius Maximianus,
>   Pious, Fortunate, Unconquered Augustus, and Flavius Valerius Constantius and
>   Galerius Valerius Maximianus, Most Noble Caesars. Aurelius Asclepiades,
>   Praeses of the Province of Arabia commanded that Castra Praetorium Mobeni (?)
>   be constructed from the foundations.
>   (Kennedy and Bewley, p. 185)

View from the north-east tower.

View from the south-east tower.

The imperial machine that willed the fort into existence was as impressive as the sonorous names and titles of its rulers. Castra Praetorium Mobeni was in commission for perhaps a century, and perhaps until the early fifth century. Its similarity in plan to the desert castles of the Umayyads means that it is not surprising that evidence of eighth-century occupation was found by the excavators.

Bshir is some 15 kilometres/9½ miles north-east of Lejjun, near the route from this to Umm ar-Rasas. It is now most easily reached by an

View from the north-west tower.

unmarked road that strikes to the north-west from the southbound carriageway of the Desert Highway a couple of kilometres/1¼ miles north of al-Qatrana. The road is metalled and on my first visit I was grateful for every kilometre – there were 10 before I reached the piste (6 miles). A sturdy fortress was visible in the far distance, four square. The track headed towards it. Then, below and to the right, Qasr Bshir came into sight. I parked on a crest, only too aware that the afternoon was drawing in and that I might not return until it was dark, and walked on for half an hour or so to the fort. Only when it is thus approached, sinking out of view as one crosses the subsidiary wadis, does one sense something of the isolation of the place.

Bshir is almost square in plan, with great projecting three-storeyed corner towers, linked by lower curtain walls. The gate, flanked by two smaller towers, is to the south-west. Within, the walls were backed by ranges on two floors: twenty-three of the twenty-six rooms on the lower level were intended for stabling, with provision — as the openings for mangers set into the walls show — for sixty-nine horses, while the upper floor, now lost, was evidently for human use. The corner towers are all ruinous. Stairways in twelve stages turned round the central square piers; and there were three rooms on each floor. One can still climb some of the stairs to look through finely cut doorways across the shattered empty rooms and survey the shadows cast by the jagged ruins on the sand. The several cisterns and the stabling are still comprehensible. So is the import of the enormous reservoir some 457 metres/500 yards to the west. This measures some 68 by 49 metres/74 by 54 yards: the walls, of thirteen visible courses that have been tactfully repointed, are some 1.75 metres/6 feet thick. Water from the wadi was deflected to a channel, in which there was an ingenious sluice, so that it could either be fed to the reservoir or put to other uses.

Whether Bshir served as a regular fort or as an occasional command post for a governor of the province of Arabia, as has been suggested, it was vulnerable to attack, whether from beyond the range of hills to the east or from the flank. So it might be thought to have needed watchtowers. In addition to that I had first seen, Qasr Abu al-Kharaq, over 3 kilometres/2 miles to the north-west, two others are visible, one small and very much reduced south of this beside the metalled road, the second, the Qasr al-Al, away to the north. Despite the failing light I could not resist making for Abu al-Kharaq, walking as fast as possible for forty-five minutes through what must once have been a more productive land than now it is, crossing wadis with ancient dams, long since silted up, and passing a single herd protected by very hostile dogs. The tower played fast and loose as I made for it. It did not disappoint, standing tall within an earlier square enclosure, apparently of Iron Age date. When the tower was built has not been established, but the evidence of shards might suggest that it is in fact rather earlier than Qasr Bshir.

The sun had sunk long before I got back to the car, perhaps 5 kilometres/3 miles away. A Bedouin who had caught me in his headlights saved me ten minutes. He was kinder than the four men in a vehicle who overtook me and then blocked me on the tarmac, convinced for some minutes that I was an Israeli. Afterwards, I fiddled with the car radio and chanced upon an Israeli channel with the news, which ended with an extract from the Queen's Christmas message – a plea for peace.

Bshir haunted me. And on my next visit to Jordan I returned, parking on this occasion by the ruined watchtower. I returned to the fort and lingered, before heading north to Qasr al-Al, knowing that it was a good deal further away than Abu al-Kharaq. I struck across a succession of small wadis, keeping to the line of a minor outpost on a ridge roughly halfway between the fort and the tower, which came into sight only as I clambered to the top of every ridge, sometimes a pale yellow in the faltering sunlight, but more often grey, against a bank of yet greyer cloud. The walk took the best part of two hours. The tower, now partly collapsed, is set at the corner of a rectangular enclosure on a ridge, which falls away to the north: occasional shafts of light caught the waves of low hills beyond the Wadi Mujib. Nothing, literally nothing, could have approached unnoticed by day from the north or the east. I planned to return by the Qasr Abu al-Kharaq, but rain decreed otherwise. A rainbow hung over the hills behind me and as I made for the car Bshir occasionally rose above the stony terrain, at times caught by the sun, at others in dark shadow or in a dramatic fusion of both light and shadow.

33. AL-QATRANA

One of the major preoccupations of the early Ottoman rulers of Syria was to monitor the pilgrimage route taken by those on the Haj from Damascus and the north, a route described in his incomparable testamentine prose by Charles Doughty, who journeyed with no fewer than 6,000 pilgrims in 1876. There are ten forts of the Ottoman period on the section of the route now in Jordan. Among the finest, just to the east of the Desert Highway, is Qasr Dab'ah, built in the sixteenth century but restored in the eighteenth. The most accessible of the Ottoman Haj forts is, however, that at Qatrana, just to the west of the Highway.

The fort was built during the reign of Suleyman the Magnificent (1520–66). Roughly square in plan, it is entered by a gate in the south wall. The fort was crenellated and machicolated, the arrowslits – four on the entrance and north walls, three each on the east and west sides

— surmounted by hood-shaped tops. The gate opens to a square space, from which — in the time-honoured way of Arab military architecture — it is necessary to turn right through a further room to reach the narrow central courtyard that runs the length of the building. Two iwans and other rooms open off this: at either end stairs climb to the upper level, with three more open rooms on the south side, and to the walkway along the battlements.

Almost more impressive than the fort itself is the huge cistern just to the east, roughly seventy-seven paces square and thus even larger than its Roman counterpart at nearby Bshir. Water was brought to this through a double-arched channel, the last section of which is in place; this fed a deep rectangular settlement tank, parallel with the south side of the cistern, which was fed through an outflow. The scale of the cistern was necessitated by the numbers of the pilgrims who passed during the Haj; but its construction, and maintenance, in the desert fringe demonstrates the priorities and administrative competence of Ottoman power at its zenith.

The fort from the reservoir.

34. KARAK

The first sight of Karak, whether from the King's Highway or the equally ancient route that climbs up the Wadi Karak from the southern end of the Dead Sea, is impressive. And the impression is not deceptive. For the castle and the walls of the town below it are among the great monuments of medieval military architecture. These crown a massive cliff-flanked promontory hanging from the southern wall of the valley, which widens as it descends to the north. To those who approached, as most Crusaders would have done, by climbing up the wadi from the west, Karak must have seemed, as the historian William of Tyre wrote, to be on 'a very high mountain'.

We from the West think of Karak as a Crusader monument. So in a sense it is. But much of what we now see is due to the Muslim rulers who succeeded where the Crusaders had failed, and whose masonry is in general more distinguished than theirs. The Crusaders, moreover, had built on a site the potential of which had long been recognized. For their Karak was the successor of the Kir-haraseth of the Moabites, and of Roman Charachmoba, the walls of which are depicted on the Madaba map.

The Crusaders advanced across the Rift Valley both for strategic and for economic reasons, establishing castles at Shobak (no. 41) and Aqaba (no. 48) in 1115 and the following year. Under King Fulk (1131–43) the Lordship of Oultrejordain was granted to Pagan the Butler, who, in 1142, decided to rule it from Karak rather than Montréal. The castle he began was strengthened by the great crusading family of de Milly, to whom this was granted in 1161. In 1177 their heiress, Etienette de Milly, married the

Walls of the castle.

brilliant but unprincipled Renaud of Châtillon, whose aggressive instincts were to do serious damage to the Crusader cause. His victory over Saladin at Montgisant in 1177 was followed a decade later by the crushing defeat of the Crusaders at Hattin, after which Renaud was personally beheaded by the Sultan, whose sense of honour he had previously outraged by breaking a truce. Already unsuccessfully invested by Saladin in 1183, Karak fell after an eight-month siege in 1188. Saladin and his Ayubbid successors reinforced the defences of Karak, and the evident impregnability of these explains why the Ayubbids held it until 1264, by when the Mamelukes had taken over much of Syria. The victorious Sultan Baybars proceeded to augment the town walls and the Mamelukes had transformed the lower bailey of the castle. The very success of the Mamelukes, who drove the Crusaders from their last coastal outposts, meant that Karak lost much of its *raison d'être*. An earthquake of 1293 caused serious damage, which was only put right in 1309. Karak remained a place of some importance to the Mamelukes. Under the Ottomans it sank into relative obscurity, from which it was briefly raised when a National Government of Moab was declared there in 1920. Recent development below the walls to the east reflects the renewed prosperity of the area.

The castle is at the narrow southern end of the outcrop. Seen from the north and east the massive glacis, recently restored, is as formidable as the towers above it. The Crusaders excavated a huge area to cut off the southern end of the fortress from the higher ground beyond. The modern road snakes up below the town walls, passing the great circular east tower, with a prominent relief of a lion, the personal symbol of Sultan Baybars, and the northern section of the walls which he greatly strengthened. The road turns through the line of the walls and into a street from which other roads run uphill to the right. The street plan is that of the Crusaders, an efficient grid adapted to the exigencies of the site. No significant early buildings survive within the town, but much work has recently been done round the square at the southern end of the town. The castle is reached from a street to the right of this.

A cutting through the rock, now largely filled in but originally as deep as its famous counterpart at Saône, divided the fortress from the town. The wall ahead is of Crusader build, put up no doubt at speed and with a view to durability rather than elegance. It is broken only by the narrow arrow slits, though which at dusk a pink sky gives an added poignancy to the cliff-like wall. The Crusaders' entrance was to the east, through a gate set into an angle of the wall, but the upper bailey of the castle is now reached though the later gate in the north-west tower.

Within the gate, the visitor can explore at will in what Sir Alec Kirkbride aptly termed 'a warren of passages and dungeons'. My inclination would be to turn left and go up to the lower of the two great corridors, or galleries, within the north wall. The original entrance gave access to this characteristic Crusader construction, partly rock cut and originally ventilated, if not lit, by three shafts from the floor of the upper gallery above. That must have been a more elegant space, with arrow slits to the north, a door and windows to the south: sections of transverse ribs

The lower bailey.

of dressed stone and areas of render survive. At the further end of the lower gallery is a smaller chamber, with, inset on the left wall, the upper part of a Nabataean funerary monument to a sturdy soldier, which must, in some way, have intrigued the Crusaders. From this chamber a narrow passage runs southwards: the wall on the right was the outer wall of the original castle, while that on the left and the room and gallery behind were built within the later extension of the east front. To the right of the passage is the kitchen. The corridor that runs from the lower north gallery was also flanked by rooms, the most interesting, on the left at the end, with a fine pointed door and on the right wall paired niches in the three vaulted sections.

The longer corridor to the west can be entered from near the gate. The rooms to the right were within the west wall of the original Crusader fortress. The corridor is continued by a narrow passage on the same alignment, which turns sharply to the left to follow the north wall of the substructure of the large chapel, the altar wall of which was built against the east wall. The vault of the chapel has largely fallen and there is, alas, no hint of the murals of a 'king in armour' and 'the martyrdom of some saint' seen by Irby and Mangles in 1818. A stair to the right of the east bay descends to the better-preserved vaulted sacristy.

A wide flight of steps by the south wall of the chapel gave access to further rooms. On the left there is a beautiful decorated block, presumably of the Mameluke period. In the room opposite it are more pillaged Nabataean fragments. Just beyond the door to this steps lead down to another corridor, built when the eastern wall of the castle was extended outwards by Renaud of Châtillon. Off this are his dungeons.

Returning to the upper level, make for the formidable keep built by the Mamelukes. The long room within this is not, at the time of writing, accessible, but steps at the west end lead to the upper level. From here one can look across the former reservoir in the great fosse cut by the Crusaders and then back across the Mameluke palace to the upper bailey, with to the west the lower bailey, which was a key element of the Mameluke contribution at Karak.

The Mameluke palace, built for Sultan al-Nasir Mohammed in 1311, is reached by a flight of steps south of the chapel. The elegant central court has iwans on the east and west sides and barrel-vaulted rooms, the doors to which are flanked by windows, at either end. A side door leads through to a room which must have been a small private mosque, as there is a mihrab or niche.

Another flight of steps from near the chapel, and a ramp below the entrance gate, both lead down to the terrace of the lower bailey, which has been well restored in recent decades. A large storeroom houses the museum: a worn lion relief, placed upside down, is just outside this. A notice on the terrace suggests that the guard at the museum will unlock the entrance to the great Mameluke galleries below. But you may have to be content with looking down through the oculus on the terrace at the remarkable cruciform hall just inside the new entrance which the Mamelukes contrived in the thirteenth century: long galleries off this run the length of the terrace. The new gate was marked externally only by two pilasters, but the elegant sophistication of the cruciform hall must have struck those who were permitted to use this ceremonial entrance. Those who entered the town from the west were no doubt equally impressed, for they had to pass through a tunnel which remained in use until the nineteenth century: the entrance to this, now blocked, is roughly 100 metres/328 feet south of the north-west tower.

Karak has changed greatly since Gertrude Bell encamped there and Kirkbride was attached to the National Government of Moab. It absorbs the tourist, yet remains a bona fide town, living not uncomfortably within the tight girdle of the walls upon which both the Crusaders and the Mamelukes expended such effort.

35. DHAT RAS

South of Karak, the King's Highway runs southwards across the Moabite plateau, passing Mu'ta, where in 629 Byzantine forces roundly defeated a small army led by Muhammed's adopted son, Zaid bin Haritha, who was among the slain. Five kilometres/3 miles further south, at al-Husayniyya, the new road diverges from the line of its predecessor for the spectacular descent to the Wadi Hasa. Turn left and then, while still in the village, right for Dhat Ras, which can be seen some 4 kilometres/2½ miles ahead on a rounded hill.

Dhat Ras was a significant Nabataean town. And the conspicuous building on the crest of the hill is one wall of a pilastered Nabataean temple, standing still to full height, yet visibly buckled by the wind, with light visible between many of the blocks. There are modern houses lower down, but the wall has been left in lonely isolation above the detritus of successive layers of the town – Nabataean, Roman and Mameluke – for there are many shards with the appealing interwoven geometrical patterns of their time.

To the south-east, in the lee of the hill, is the fenced-off archaeological area round the very well-preserved temple Roman temple. There is no sign of a guardian. And men at the bakery nearby tell me to climb in. I do, feeling rather conspicuous as schoolchildren take an interest, half remembering that when I was here twenty years earlier their parents had amused themselves by covering the windows of the car Simon and I had hired with messages in Arabic that we could not read, but which evidently gave them a good deal of satisfaction.

The temple is a counterpart to that at Rabba. It is set on a podium, the relatively recently excavated lower blocks of which have been less exposed than those higher up. The entrance is on the south, the portal flanked by arched niches, the sides with shallow pilasters. In the cella, opposite the door, is a generous recess set within a high arch: at either side there are pairs of blank arches that rest on single central supports. The cornice above the central arch is continued horizontally above the level of the arches of the lateral walls. A door in the central recess leads to stairs up to the upper level: a break in the wall on the west makes it possible to see into the barrel-vaulted upper room.

Wall of the Nabatean temple.

The temple was no doubt positioned to make the maximum impact on the traveller who had taken the King's Highway from the south, climbing up from the crossing of the Wadi Hasa by way of Al'Aina and Shurqairah, another Nabataean site with a reservoir that has been brought back into use.

36. KHIRBET TANNUR
and QASR ADH-DHARITH

The Nabataeans, more perhaps than many ancient peoples, understood the magic of wild places. This is evident not only in their choice of such sites as Sela and Sheikh ar-Rishi, but also in that of their High Places, not least at Petra. So it is not surprising that they were drawn to Khirbet Tannur, the striking hill south of the Wadi Hasa, which answers the black flank of an extinct volcano to the north and seems to dominate the King's Highway in both directions.

An altar was placed on the summit in the first century BC, but the temple itself, and with the annexed buildings, was only completed in the second century AD. The remains were excavated in the 1930s and now all that can be seen are footings of walls and scattered blocks. There was, no doubt, a processional approach up the steep hillside from the south-east. A gateway on the east led to the rectangular paved precinct, within which to the right there is an altar, alas largely destroyed, and the pilastered temple ahead: within this there was an inner shrine. The precinct was surrounded by three ranges of buildings, that to the north with two of the triclinia that had so important a place in the social life of the Nabataeans; a third adjoined these but was entered from outside the precinct, which may imply some hierarchy as to who could use the three rooms. Among the fallen blocks are sections of friezes and characteristic Nabataean capitals, of an austere abbreviated form that is partly derived from the Corinthian order. The relief of Atargatis, the Syrian goddess who subsumed many of the attributes of Hera, Aphrodite and Cybele, now at Amman but originally above the door of the temple, is not a great work of art, but must have had a strange power in this elevated setting. But her devotees could not

Qasr adh-Dharith: a capital.

afford to neglect the practical: there is an efficient drain in the corner of the precinct.

Hardly 5 kilometres/3 miles to the south is another Nabataean temple, better preserved if less spectacularly placed, on a shelf above the east bank of the subsidiary Wadi La'ban and near a perennial spring. The ruins are reached from a rough road to the left of the King's Highway. Qasr adh-Dharith is so similar in some respects to the temple on Khirbet Tannur that it has been suggested that the same craftsmen worked on both.

The temple was set in a substantial temenos, much of the wall of which survives. Within this, on the west side of the temple, part of the arched subterranean corridor that supported the paving of the precinct is in place; its counterpart on the north, originally with ten arched ribs, has fallen. To the east of the temple there is a square altar of particularly finely cut blocks. The temple was entered from the south, its façade enriched with engaged columns. The gate opens to an outer space, the inner wall of which was partly filled in when the temple was adapted as a church in Byzantine times, and the existing door, with a cross on the lintel, was inserted. To the right of this there is a Nabataean niche. Ahead is the colonnaded cella, with columns grafted together at the corners. The front is richly carved with plant forms, the capitals with lion heads that may allude to the all-embracing cult of Atargatis.

Steps lead up to the central chamber, and the narrow passage that runs round the outer wall of the cella gives access to two small rooms behind it in the centre. The Byzantines seem to have used the east arm of the space in front of the cella as the apse of a church, but happily did no significant damage to the cella.

The structures to the south of the temple were for the most part Byzantine, but reused early material. Of particular interest is the plant for processing olive oil, which demonstrates that olives were then grown in the wadi, as is now once again the case. Near by sections of friezes and other decorated blocks were laid out by the excavators. These confirm one's sense that the temple must have been among the most elegant of Nabataean buildings. What it may have lacked of the solemn and disciplined coherence of the temple at Al Qasr is more than made up for by the quality of its decoration. Despite the proximity of the road, the temple sits easily in the valley: the stone takes on the colour of the wadi itself, that of pale, very milky coffee.

37. SELA

Even in country as dramatic as that of the wadis that drain to the Rift Valley, the Nabataean outpost of Sela must always have seemed out of the ordinary. Today, as we turn off the King's Highway and snake down to the abandoned village of Sela with its houses, four square, of stone, we are almost uncomfortably aware of the plunging depths below. The road continues downwards. A herdsman crosses with his sheep and four small boys hover, enjoying the afternoon sun. The sharp outcrop appropriated by the Nabataeans is seen below the escarpment on the north. The road peters out before a group of rocks, one with a cutting in its eastern face, and a path leads to the left through these:

Rock-cut houses on the summit.

Nabataean steps ease the descent and we turn to see the outcrop at closer quarters, its cliffs separated by a vertical fissure. To the left, high on the rock, difficult to see without field glasses and in morning light, is a Babylonian relief with a cuneiform inscription that has no counterpart in the area.

The path descends to a stream bed – there is the remnant of a characteristic Nabataean dam in a subsidiary channel immediately to the right. Cross to the fissure in which successive flights of steps, some wider, some narrow, climb and turn as the rock dictated. Towards the summit, where the steps widen out and turn to the left towards a low cliff, there is a choice of routes. Steps to the right run up to the top of the outcrop, where the main settlement lay, while those on the left mount to what must have been the gatehouse, with a small bastion of rock on the left topped by a wall, now much crumbled. Holes in the rock show where the way was barred. Scramble up behind the rock to gain what was evidently a walled enclosure, at the eastern angle of which, beetling above the cliff, was a small house. Part of the rock-cut roof of this survives to protect faint traces of the original decoration in red and green. In front of the house was a cistern, and everywhere there is evidence of the efficiency with which the Nabataeans conserved such rainwater as there was.

Climb over the rocks to the west, or take the steps opposite those up to the gate, to reach the summit of the hill. This was intensively occupied in Nabataean times. The numerous protrusions of the rock were put to use: rooms were built into them and holes for roof timbers tell of lost structures – a flight of steps here, cisterns there. Near one of these there is an Islamic contribution, a particularly carefully cut gameboard, with two rows of seven small holes and behind the third from the left on each side a larger circular cut. Inevitably two millennia of erosion, not least by wind, have taken their toll. So much is left to the imagination.

Sela is a magical place. I have been twice in the afternoon: the Babylonian relief is all but invisible, but the rocks are suffused with the failing light, the hillsides above touched with pink. Knowing that a tourist's car is still below them, the boys have lingered in expectation of a lift. For them it is of course irrelevant whether Sela, which means rock in Hebrew, is the place of that name referred to in the Book of Kings where King Amaziah of Judah despatched 10,000 Edomites or, as Diodorus records, where the women and children of the Nabataeans took refuge in 312 BC. In my opinion neither identification is at all plausible.

38. BUSAYRA

Relatively few tourists trouble to see Busayra. But as it lies hardly 4 kilometres/2½ miles off the King's Highway it seems almost perverse to pass by what remains of Bozrah, the capital of the Edomites. Isaiah had very energetic views about the place, perhaps because in its brief history, from the seventh century BC until after the Persian occupation of 539 BC, Bozrah was enviably prosperous, as the kingdom of Edom controlled the all-important copper deposits of the hills to the west.

The modern town of Busayra has little but position to commend it. And there is no evidence that anyone wished to salvage such of the early houses as survive, as is happening in the nearby village of Dana. At the end of the town, encroached upon by a school, is the promontory site which the Edomites clearly chose with an eye to defence. Parts of this have been excavated, and although the place now seems rather abandoned and forlorn, it exerts a potent fascination.

Park by the school and walk up to the left of this. Just within the gate is a group of buildings, Area C, that have been excavated. The most intriguing of the rooms that can be seen, approached through two smaller rooms, has been identified as a bathroom, as there is a substantial basin in the north-west corner: beside this is a hole which has more surprisingly been thought to be a lavatory. Further on, behind the school buildings, at the highest point of the promontory, was the so-called acropolis. This consisted of two large rectangular buildings, the earlier of which lies to the west. The walls were constructed of massive if irregular blocks, as can best be seen at the northern corners. To the east of this was a wide flight of steps, much affected by fire, linking it with a court.

The importance of Edomite Bozrah is demonstrated best not by these buildings but by the enceinte of the city walls. The southern line has been lost, but the rest can still be followed, although in many areas only battered footings survive. The layout, determined by the shape of the hill, was roughly rectangular, some 250 metres/820 feet in length and 100 metres/328 feet in width to the south, tapering to little more than 60 metres/197 feet at the north end. To the west of the 'acropolis' is a substantial gate, which has been excavated. The wall itself at this point was some 3.5 metres/12 feet thick, with roughly hewn shaped blocks on the outer faces and smaller infilling between; but additional buildings were added behind the wall, so that those who entered had to negotiate a long and relatively narrow entrance passage. The footway to this was raised and, to control access to the gate from outside, the wall was stepped forward by 60 centimetres/24 inches a little to the north. The same device was employed on the northern line of the walls in at least two places. The importance attached to the device is suggested by the carefully graded stones that remain in place in the undamaged example. The highest extant section of the wall is at the north-east corner, where the ground has recently been cleared for a road, and serves to remind us to how much effort the Edomites had to go to in order to protect their hard-won riches from envious neighbours.

The north wall.

39. DANA: SHEIKH AR-RISHI

Height held no fear for the Nabataeans. Nowhere perhaps is one more aware of this than at Sheikh ar-Rishi ('canyon of the feathers'), an almost inaccessible fastness in a rash of protrusions that seem to erupt from the mountainside as one looks downwards across them from a minor road off that which descends to the much-visited village of Dana. The whole area is within the Dana Nature Reserve, and so presumably protected for posterity. Personal experience has proved that it can be surprisingly difficult to arrange for a guide through the Dana Visitor Centre: the enterprising Suleiman Jarad of the Dana Hotel, who is one of the key figures in the campaign to find new uses for the old stone buildings of the village, is altogether more dependable. And it should absolutely be stressed that without a local guide, finding the ways across the rocks would be a slow, painful and, quite possibly, dangerous process.

The most rewarding route cuts down just below a small military post, circling to the left of the rocks, before cutting down a path between these, and continuing downwards through a series of open areas linked by gullies, before turning northwards towards Sheikh ar-Rishi itself, which is cut off from an equally substantial outcrop to the east by a wide chasm. The first obvious sign of Nabataean activity is a large rock at the southern end of the outcrop, the surface of which has been neatly quarried away at an angle perhaps five degrees from the vertical. Beside it is a small cave, now apparently used by wild cats, and small areas of the rock are pink and yellow. The path continues round the east face of the rock. Soon vestigial walls appear above and to the left, and the path turns, up recognizably Nabataean steps, to a wide sloping terrace, on which there evidently was a substantial settlement. This is littered with the detritus of

Nabataean walls, and in the rocks that enclose it there are numerous cuttings, one small protrusion bearing well over twenty holes for roof timbers. A cleft to the left leads to a smaller clearing, with more signs of habitation.

At the upper end of the terrace the way follows up a natural gap between the rocks, with steps and more holes for roof timbers. Higher up a wholly artificial cutting through the ridge of rock on the left leads by a turning, which should be treated with respect, to a fissure, or siq, which the Nabataeans characteristically enhanced, running steeply upwards almost to the top of the outcrop. Almost immediately on the right a door opens to a small oval rock-cut room, lit by a small window. There are several more such excavations on the way up, the doors of most protected from erosion by channelling to deflect rain.

The natural protrusions on the crests of the outcrop were put to ingenious use. Many of the higher rocks have elaborate cuttings for water catchment, in some cases reached by flights of steps. There are numerous rounded cisterns, of varying size. Some of the excavated rooms were relatively elaborate: in one on the east side there is a niche opposite the door with a smaller one to the right, with two lesser spaces and smaller recesses, a second niche on the narrower left wall and, to the right of the door, a sunken basin below the window. Elsewhere there are doors with recesses for fixings and bolts. Between the rocks there is a scattering of shards: the odd small purplish colchicum is in flower, as if to remind us that the wild onions with their luridly green leaves are not the only plants to hold out against the prolonged drought. The wind is relentless, but even on a clouded morning the views over the eroded rocks and down to the Wadi Dana are remarkable. So it was with some reluctance that I made my way down to the terrace below, where my guide had long since made tea.

We returned by a different route, making through the rocks to the east, up a fissure in which the Nabataeans had cut steps where necessary, and at one point built a small dam, presumably to serve the inhabitants of the terrace round to the right where there are traces of more houses. Sheikh ar-Rishi cannot vie with the ceremonial approach of Sela, and was, by the standards of Petra, little more than a village. But it offers a precious microcosm of a long-vanished world.

The siq.

40. DA'JANIYA

Not everyone shares my fascination for Roman fortresses. Qasr Bshir sets an Olympian standard. And Da'janiya cannot match it. But it is nonetheless a rather remarkable survival, more complete than any of the Hadrianic forts in Britain and with few equals even in the Near East. It lies a few kilometres to the west of the Desert Highway, on a low rise in level country, and is most easily reached from a turn marked to Rawad Ameer some 5 kilometres/3 miles north of that for Shobak. The fort is easily made out, a low mass of masonry in shadow against the almost ubiquitous brown of the terrain, scarcely 2 kilometres/1¼ miles south of the road. And when the sun is behind it, one is less uncomfortably aware of the one drawback of the recent consolidation of the basalt walls: the fact that too pale a cement was used.

Da'janiya from the north.

The fort is square in plan, roughly 100 metres/328 feet across. There were substantial projecting towers at the corners and two smaller ones between them, except on the south-east side, at the centre of which was the main gate, flanked by two lateral towers. A road crossed to the smaller gate on the north-west wall. On this were barrack blocks and a headquarters building, while other structures were ranged against the outer walls. Almost everything has fallen. One surveys a mass of rough black stones, long since detached from the cemented hard core that they formerly faced. But slowly the eye works out the rough forms of the buildings these represent. Da'janiya was not a place for architectural refinement. There are no inscriptions, no scattered column drums or fragments of carved cornices. Dressed stone was used with economy where it was necessary: it can thus be seen in what survives of the jambs of the north-west gate and in the arched postern by the southern interval tower on the south-west wall.

We do not know when the fort was built, although a date in the third or fourth centuries is probable. But we can still understand why it was placed where it is. For from the walls one can still watch a wide swathe of country, control of which was a prerequisite for the effectiveness of Rome's Limes Arabicus, her border with the Arab hinterland.

While Lejjun was served by a perennial spring, Da'janiya had no such advantage. A substantial cistern was cut into the bedrock just within the north-west gate, but a fort of this size required a good deal more. Water that ran in the wadi to the south after rain was deflected to a very substantial cistern south of the fort. The cistern has now, alas, been encased in concrete, but its original form has been preserved. The continuing availability of water at the fort must explain why it was frequented by the Bedouin in the nineteenth century, as that most austere of Victorian travellers Charles Doughty recorded.

41. SHOBAK: MONTREAL

The formidable fortress of Shobak is happily separated from the modern town of that name, which lies on the King's Highway, by a ridge; and the inevitable visitor centre apart, its context has not been disturbed, although the oak forests seen by Doughty have sadly long been felled. The site is a steep conical hill – in Lawrence's words a 'shapely cone' – that stands forward from the escarpment: to the north the land falls away in a series of valleys that drain through the gorge of the Wadi Ghuweir to Feinan and the Wadi Araba. King Baldwin I, characteristically alert to strategic potential, ordered the construction of the castle of Montréal in 1115, paying homage in doing so to the Byzantines, who had built more modest defences there half a millennium earlier. Montréal became the centre of the Crusader Lordship of Oultrejourdain, until Pagan the Butler transferred his administration to Karak. Despite the priority given to the reinforcement of the latter, it was Montréal that held out for longer after the debacle of Hattin, thanks in part to its water supply, only surrendering in 1189. Saladin entrusted it to his brother and further work was done under his Ayyubid successors. These in their turn were defeated by the Mameluke Sultan Baybars. He also reinforced the castle. Severely damaged in the 1293 earthquake, this was restored under Sultan Hasam al-Din Lajin (1297–8). Much of what can now be seen is of these post-Crusader phases. Shobak continued to be occupied, eventually sheltering a village. Until this was cleared some fifty years ago, none of the internal structures except the well shaft could be seen. A major programme of restoration was begun in 1999.

The most impressive approach is from the north, by way of Mansourah, but Shobak is more usually reached from above. The road from the town cuts downwards, passing the visitor centre. Beyond this a narrow lane strikes up the hill to the gate, to the right of which is a tower in excellent bossed masonry, the inscription on which mentions Hasam al-Din Lajin. The outer gate itself is less impressive. Further on, to the left, approached through a room of indeterminate function above a cistern and at a lower level, is the partly reconstructed barrel-vaulted chapel. Although not large, this was a building of some distinction, with an apse, the cornice of which is continued over the two small niches on the adjacent right wall. Steps indicate the position

Thirteenth-century inscription on the southern tower.

of the original west door through which the chapel would have been entered. Returning to the main path you reach what was the original entrance. To the right of the path, before a short flight of steps, is the door to the remarkable tunnelled well shaft, down which about 375 steps descend to a cistern fed by a natural spring at the level of the foot of the hill. Near the top, the path turns to the right and continues more or less on the same alignment, but narrowing perceptibly, for what even

The chapel.

with a good torch seems a considerable way, to a pointed arch: at this point narrow and more vertiginous steps run down to the right, but fallen debris mean that care has to be taken. These stairs were Montréal's lifeline during the eighteen-month siege of 1187–9.

It is a relief to escape from the dust and return to the circuit, which continues with a long passage, from which one can enter some of the post-Crusader fortifications, with fine recessed arrow slits. The most impressive of these interiors is at the south. On my first visit it was raining gently and I tried to take an undistorted photograph, leaning into a corner: fortunately I was quick, for within a few seconds of my walking forwards the cornerstone of the vault fell, as if to tell me that ruins should be treated with respect. Look at the admirable bossed masonry of the outer wall of the tower, before cutting to the right to examine the very remarkable remains of an Ayyubid palace. At the centre of this is a great ceremonial hall, in three sections, with iwans on the north and south sides. The way in which the masonry is carried up into the converging vaults is particularly satisfying.

Much work has recently been done on the complex, and this is also the case with the substantial church on the western side of the enceinte. Because of the position the church was not orientated. The main entrance is thus on the cut, flanked by subsidiary doors to the aisles. The generously proportioned nave is separated from the aisles at either side by two piers with projecting ribs that would have run up to the vaults: a cornice that is stepped above the arches binds the elements of an appropriately austere design. But much is left to the imagination and the choir has fallen away. The substructure, in part of which decorated blocks and querns from the castle are now stored, is, however, substantially intact.

Interior of the southern Mameluke tower.

42. 'UDRUH

As Montréal was the Crusaders' main military base between Karak and Aqaba, so the fortress at 'Udruh on the Via Nova Traiana, some 25 kilometres/15½ miles to the south, was the key Roman fortress in the area. When the Nabataean kingdom was absorbed in AD 106, Trajan lost little time in projecting the military road that was to take his name; and work began on the defences at 'Udruh, which was probably the Roman Augustopolis and thus presumably named after the first emperor. The fortress succeeded a settlement of the Nabataean period, which had grown up beside what was already a much-frequented trade route between Azraq and the north. The position on the flank of a hill sloping to the east had obvious advantages: a natural spring, commanding views and the ability both to control the approach from the desert to the former Nabataean capital of Petra, some 16 kilometres/10 miles to the west, and to discourage local dissidence.

The lie of the ground meant that 'Udruh was laid out not on a square or rectangular plan but as a trapeze, with its shortest side on the high ground at the top of the hill to the west; while the north and south walls, again taking advantage of the terrain, fan out in their descent to the longer east wall, which is just above the bottom of the slope. At the corners there are substantial projecting circular towers: of these that at the north-west is the most impressive. The walls were further strengthened with a total of twenty smaller rounded towers. These may belong to a subsequent building campaign, as they were not bonded into the walls.

Although a good deal of work has been done at 'Udruh, the site is in some ways rather confusing. A layer of earth perhaps 4.5 metres/15 feet deep has been partly cleared from the east wall, and many buildings associated with this presumably survive to first-floor level. But much

The Ottoman fort.

material must have been taken for the modern village to the north and east, a process begun much earlier, when a substantial fort was built against the north wall: with its arched entrance from the south and rooms off a central court, this closely resembles the series of sixteenth-century Ottoman Haj forts and presumably is of similar date. Some of the original blocks in the wall are massive – I noticed one perhaps 3.35 metres/11 feet long and 1 metre/3 feet high. The west section is the most impressive, with substantial remains of a gate and of both flanking and corner towers. That at the south-west corner was evidently kept in commission well into the Arab period. I saw little of this on my first visit, as snow settled on the walls. But more recently, as I picked my way down though the ruins towards the unkempt excavated remains of the principia, which was remodelled in Byzantine days as a church, the sun caught a gleaming fragment of white marble facing, which hinted at former luxury. Yet 'Udruh must always have seemed an austere place to those en route to or from its western neighbour, Petra.

43. PETRA

Petra is, of course, the most celebrated site of Jordan. And its celebrity is wholly deserved. This is owed in part to the setting, a wide valley to the east of the Wadi Araba that opens between two chains of cliff-flanked hills which are cut by deep wadis. Water in a land where it is not abundant brought animals and thus men in pursuit of these from early times, and by about 7000 BC a farming community was established at Beidha (no. 44). This was eventually abandoned. In the seventh century BC the Edomites occupied the hanging plateau on the summit of Umm al-Biyara, which dominates the site of the future city, and established a settlement near 'Ain Musa, the spring below the flank of the escarpment to the east. Despite their wealth, they, like their neighbours, succumbed to empires from the east, but by the late fourth century BC much of their territory was held by the Nabataeans, a people of Arab origin who controlled much of the crucial trade in spices and frankincense from what the Romans were to term Arabia Felix. In about 312 BC Antigonus, a former general of Alexander, sent two successive armies to deal with the Nabataeans: both failed.

When the Nabataeans established their monarchy remains uncertain: the first recorded king, Aretas I, reigned in about 168 BC, by when a Nabataean trading presence had long been established in the lands to the north. Trade was central to the evolution of the Nabataean state, and it is perhaps not wholly mistaken to suggest a parallel between the emergence of its royal line and that of the Medici, who rose to power on the strength of their success as bankers. Despite their nomad roots, and the seasonal nature of the vital trade from the south, Petra became the Nabataeans' capital, not least because it was so ideally placed to serve as an entrepôt.

The first century BC saw the kingdom at its zenith, but already Pompey's annexation of Syria may have seemed an alarming portent. The Nabataeans wisely allied themselves with Rome, but in the following century were unable to prevent the deflection of much of the Red Sea trade, which they had effectively monopolized, to ports in Egypt that were under Roman control. King Rabbel II (70–106) succeeded to the throne in changing circumstances, basing himself mainly at Bosra rather than Petra. On his death, perhaps as a result of a prior arrangement, his realm was incorporated in the Roman Empire by the Emperor Trajan. Petra remained a city of considerable importance, but Bosra was the capital of the province of Arabia, and the Via Nova Traiana, on which both the defences and much of the trade of Roman Syria passed, ran some 15 kilometres/9½ miles to the east. In the Byzantine era Petra was still the seat of a bishop, but after the Arab conquest decline set in. The Crusaders, intent on taxing passing traffic and protecting their lines of communication, built two fortresses, Al Wu'eira to the east and on Al Habis above the centre of the city. But thereafter Petra disappears from view. Jealously guarded by local tribes, the ruins were only rediscovered in 1812 by John Lewis Burckhardt, who was in the service of the London-based Association for Promoting the Discovery of the Interior Parts of Africa. His find fired the public imagination. Later travellers followed, and few places have been examined more thoroughly. Petra continues to yield its secrets, and as a result of recent excavations we can now see more clearly that the celebrated rock-cut monuments were matched by the buildings constructed in the heart of the city.

In Petra's heyday most caravans would have arrived either from the south or from the north, rather than from the east through the siq – the gorge carved through a natural fault by the waters of the Wadi Musa – which most visitors take today from the unprepossessing modern town that takes the name of the wadi, with its numerous hotels and tourist facilities which have the merit of relieving pressure on the ancient city.

The siq was, however, unquestionably the ceremonial approach to the city. It has perhaps no equal.

Beyond the visitor centre is the Bab as-Siq, the 'gate to the siq', where the valley narrows. The path above the right bank of the wadi, which is normally dry, curls gently to the right. The Nabataeans, like other ancient peoples, knew how funerary monuments could be placed to dignify the approaches to great cities, and did so with spectacular effect here, exploiting a sequence of outcrops which were quarried away. The three large square blocks on the right, the so-called djinn blocks, set the tone. Across the stream bed there are cuttings and associated tombs, and then, higher up, the splendid Obelisk Tomb, the façade of which is enriched with four obelisks: this was the tomb of 'Abdmank, as inscriptions in both Nabataean and Greek attest, and may be of the first century. Below, but not strictly aligned on the tomb, is the façade of a triclinium (AD 25–75).

Back on the right bank there are further tombs, as well as the Aslah Triclinium, with an inscription dating it to the reign of King Obodas I (96/92–86 BC). The wadi opens out to the left, with small terraced fields, through which a path climbs to the cliff-top suburb of Al-Madras, only to close in again. Here a modern bridge crosses to the siq from which the wadi was diverted by the Nabataeans northwards through a tunnel to join the narrow Wadi Mughlim, which is an alternative but much longer route round the Jebel al-Khubtha, and thus to the Wadi Mataha and the centre of the city: just beyond the tunnel a subsidiary wadi descends from the left, with, on the right, a cluster of niches, one of which is carved with an eagle.

The siq is in some ways the ultimate statement of the Nabataeans' very understandable obsession with controlling the water resources of their land. Protected from flash floods, the canyon sculpted by the wadi was cleared of obstructions and carefully levelled with a paved road surface,

The Deir.

much of which survives, sloping gradually downwards. Small dams, some of which have been rebuilt, caught water from the minor subsidiary wadis; and a channel on the left directed this towards the city. The entrance to the siq was marked by a great arch which was recorded by Laborde and Roberts but has long since fallen: the surviving abutments and lower courses of the arch proper give an idea of the size of what may be seen as a monumental gateway to the siq.

The siq, which is over a kilometre/four-fifths of a mile long, clearly had a practical function as a road; but as the numerous votive niches with god blocks (rectangular carvings representing deities) demonstrate, it had also a strong religious significance. It was indeed treated as a place of pilgrimage, as is shown by the inscription on a relief of a god between two animals, some 411 metres/450 yards down the siq on the left, which was dedicated to the principal Nabataean deity, Dushara, by one Sabinos Alexandros, who presided over religious festivals at Adraa (Deraa, now in Syria) and evidently sought to commemorate his visit to Petra. The siq twists and turns, widening in places and then narrowing. The vertical walls draw the eye upwards. Sounds echo. The magic of the place is most intense in the early morning, when few other tourists are about, or at dusk. Our experience may be coloured by a Western European sense of the picturesque and the romantic; but this should not make us doubt that the Nabataeans were equally moved by the strange beauty of the place, and saw their passage through the siq as a prelude to their progression to one or other of the High Places where they worshipped their gods. Only such a conviction perhaps can explain the spectacular finale: the walls of the siq close in as it turns to disclose the unforgettable first sight of a narrow section of the façade of the best-known monument of Petra, the so-called Treasury. For Gertrude Bell, who was not given to hyperbole, this was 'the most beautiful sight' she had ever seen. And one can understand why.

The Treasury was most probably a funerary monument, of the first century BC. It was cut back into the pinkish sandstone of the cliff, and dominates an irregular open area, surrounded by cliffs except to the south, where a long flight of steps climbs bravely upwards. The portico in antis is surmounted by a columned tholos crowned by an urn, and by a broken pediment supported on matching columns. But this bare description gives no hint of the subtlety of the composition, which is given a proto-baroque sense of movement by the spacing of the columns. The atrium, with a small room on each side, leads to a large chamber, off which are three smaller rooms, on the back wall of the innermost of which many early visitors had their names cut. Partly because it is so well protected from the wind, the architectural detail of the façade is beautifully preserved; but the sculpture – reliefs of the Dioscuri flanking the portico and figures, including winged victories, and eagles above – is more battered. The two rows of holes at either side of the monument were clearly made to facilitate the quarrying of the rock. As recent excavations have shown, the ground level was originally considerably lower.

The Treasury was placed to impress, and to serve as it were as a frontispiece to one of the most spectacular of ancient necropoli. The wadi bed, now wider and usually referred to as the outer siq, continues to the right, gradually opening out. There is a cluster of rather ponderous monuments on the left, and beyond these, ranged on four levels, the so-called Street of Tombs, many of the façades of which are enriched with one or two rows of the crowsteps that were the Nabataean equivalents of classical acroteria. On the opposite, north, wall of the outer siq there are other substantial tombs, worth visiting not least to escape from the vendors whose stalls line the wadi floor. The finest of the group are perhaps no. 813, a little way up – originally entered through a porticoed court with an associated triclinium – which may have been the tomb of Unaishu, who is stated in an inscription to have been the brother of Queen Shuqailat, and no. 808, a fine example of the so-called double-cornice type, with sharply cut angle pilasters: chisel marks are still clearly visible on the façade. From the top of the cliff in front of the tomb there is a splendid view over the outer siq and down to the first-century theatre, which is of Hellenistic type and would have accommodated an audience of over six thousand. The cavea was largely excavated from the cliff, ruthlessly obliterating earlier tombs, as cuttings above the upper row of benches show.

A path from Tomb 808 leads round to the so-called Royal Tombs carved into the west face of the Jebel al-Khubtha, and placed to be seen from the centre of the city. First, approached by a stair beside the partly reconstructed barrel-vaulted substructure of the splendid forecourt, of which the lateral rock-cut colonnades survive, is the Urn Tomb. The chamber of this was ingeniously adapted as a church in 341: holes in the floor indicate the positions of the screen of the chancel and other fixtures. From the forecourt there are commanding views over Petra. A little to the north, side by side and almost on the axis of the colonnaded street that continues from the siq, are the Corinthian and Palace Tombs. Both are large and rather repetitive in design, the former with its tholos an overblown counterpart to the Treasury, the latter with a lugubrious façade in five tiers, which is best preserved on the right where it has been less exposed to the wind.

One interesting tomb, that of Sextius Florentinus, which would not have looked out of place in Renaissance Italy, is some way to the north on the flank of the jebel, and there are numerous other cuttings both in this and on the low hill on the other side of the Wadi Mataha, Mughur an Nasara. But those with only two or three days in hand should walk down to the former course of the Wadi Musa and make for the Colonnaded Street, the main artery of Petra. This was flanked by some of the major monuments of the city and led up to the gate to the temenos of the main temple of the city, the Qasr al-Bint. Only the foundations survive of the first of the public buildings, the nymphaeum on the right, where the Wadi Mataha, reinforced by the water deflected from the siq, cuts down from the north-east. Just beyond this there is a footbridge across the wadi, from which a path leads upwards to the substantial late fifth-century church, which was subsequently remodelled but abandoned after a fire in about 600. This was entered from a colonnaded atrium, on the west side of which is a baptistery, with a cross-shaped font. The church is most notable for the mosaics of the aisles: in that on the left there is a design of scrolling vines framing twenty-eight rows of three compartments of which those in the centre, mostly of objects, are flanked by paired roundels, of which the majority represent animals. We are indeed presented with a veritable bestiary. Two other churches are further to the north, but within the line of the city walls.

Return to the Colonnaded Street. This is aligned on the south bank of the wadi. On the rising ground to the left were two market complexes, and beyond these the Garden Terrace, an early exemplar of the Arabs' passion for plants and water. Adjoining this is one of the signal monuments of Petra, the recently excavated Great Temple. The propylaeum at street level led to a wide flight of steps up to the huge Lower Terrace, paved with hexagons and flanked by double colonnades with rather uncomfortably placed exedras at their southern ends. Three flights of steps mounted to the Upper Temenos, with a small theatre within the cella, and further steps to a landing at the back of this. Most remarkably sections of original *trompe l'oeil* pigmentation survive, with strong tones of red, yellow, green and blue; so do sections of the plaster decoration of the columns. Work began in the first century BC and progressed in subsequent campaigns: repairs were undertaken after an earthquake of 113–14, for the Romans were assiduous at promoting the deities of the peoples they ruled; a further earthquake struck in 363, but the temple was not immediately abandoned. Descending from the Great Temple there is an excellent view of the Temple of the Winged Lion or al-Uzza, of the first century AD, on the north bank of the wadi, which was originally approached from a platform built out across this. The relatively modest cella was flanked by colonnades, and the complex included a number of shops.

The Colonnaded Street ends just beyond the two temples at the partly restored Temenos Gate, with three arches that were originally closed by doors. Here the pilgrim reached the precinct of the massive late first-century AD Nabataean temple that was presumably dedicated to Dushara, now known as the Qasr al-Bint al-Faraoun ('palace of the daughter of Pharoah'), which is some 137 metres/150 yards ahead, to the left of a large altar on which it was aligned. A wide flight of steps, originally faced in marble, led up to a portico in antis: the huge central portal in the wall behind this, the relieving arch of which survives, opened to the cella, with a central adyton between two wider ones, entered originally through screens of columns. Enough of the original plaster decoration survives to give some sense of the intended richness of the interior. Stairs from the lateral adytons led to the upper level, and it is instructive to climb those from that on the west, both to savour the quality of the ashlar masonry and to look up at El Habis, the outcrop that literally hangs above the temple and clearly dictated its placing.

To the north of the temple, across the wadi and near the restaurant, is a small museum. There is a sharply cut sphinx in sandstone, found on the Colonnaded Street, and a third-century Venus of marble from the theatre. The selection of Nabataean pottery is comprehensive, with a number of vessels decorated with palmettes, and a bowl painted with two birds.

The visitor to Petra should try to see as many of the peripheral sites as time allows. All these involve a considerable amount of walking, and care needs to be taken. Architecturally the Deir and the High Place on the Jebel al-Madbah above the theatre are the most remarkable. But there is a case for starting, ideally in the cool of the morning, with El Habis. There are numerous tombs on the east face of the outcrop, behind the Qasr al-Bint, including the Unfinished Tomb, the carving of which was begun from the top. A good path, with steps and at one point a footbridge, climbs to the Crusaders' fortalice on the crest: this was evidently an outstation of their more substantial fortress of Al Wu'eira to the east. On the north side of the outcrop, across the Wadi Siyyagh from the museum, is a sunken courtyard, the so-called Convent, which may have been associated with a small High Place above a crowstepped tomb. Following the wadi to the west there is a scattering of tombs. One is almost surprised by the virulence of vegetation. Ahead, where the Wadi Kharrubal Ibn Jurayma comes in from the left, the Wadi Siyyagh turns sharply to the right, and is fringed by walled enclosures with trees. But it is less for these than for the Nabataean quarries, cut into the cliffs, that the walk is memorable. Some half a mile beyond the undercut quarry on the right wall of the canyon is the dripping well which must always have been held in reverence.

The energetic may opt not by retrace their steps to the area of the

Quarried cliff in the Wadi Siyyagh.

museum but to follow the Wadi Kharrubal Ibn Jurayma to the spectacular group of tombs and houses on the eastern flank of Umm al-Biyara ('mother of cisterns'), the mountain that towers above Petra from the west. Best seen in the morning, the tombs are most readily accessible from a path that cuts south-east from the Qasr al-Bint to an isolated column, Amud Faraoun ('Pharoah's phallus'), and then strikes south-west. To the left of the main cluster of monuments on the lower part of the cliff is the couloir through which the processional route begins the ascent. The way is marked with cairns but on my first visit I took a guide. Stairs, once dignified with an arch, rise to a passage that turns back and leads to two ramps: take that to the south. The familiar Nabataean steps exploit every feature of the terrain, turning and cutting, and descend only once before resuming the upward trail. In places they are badly worn, and it is as well to scramble on all fours, the precipice at one's side: mercifully vertigo does not run in my family. The views are wonderful, and near the top the Jebel Haroun comes into sight.

The massif tilts downwards from the west. We followed the crest, looking down towards the Wadi Araba across bastions of rock moated by deep wadis, country so impenetrable that Ishmael enjoyed himself hurling quite large stones and listening as they crashed and crashed again far below. From the highest point we crossed to the excavated area – seventh-century BC Edomite walls of no great visual merit but nobly set – and it was only on a later visit that I found my way to the superbly placed Nabataean sanctuary at the north-west angle of the mountain. Near the eastern edge there are cisterns, probably of Nabataean date. The provision of water must always have been a problem, and if Umm al-Biyara was the biblical Sela (see no. 37), it is difficult to see how 10,000 people could have expected to survive there for any length of time. The views over Petra itself are less informative than those from El Habis,

Quarry below the High Place.

but not the less memorable for that. On the descent I was distracted by the extraordinary beauty of the country in the sharp clear light, and slipped: nothing dangerous but a cut in my hand bled enthusiastically. Ishmael insisted on cauterizing it with ash from his cigarette: the quick pain certainly stopped the bleeding.

The High Place can be reached from a path that climbs from near the theatre and by the processional route from the Wadi Farasa on the west, just beyond the line of the southern stretch of the city wall. The importance of the processional route to the Nabataeans is implied by the distinction of some of the monuments associated with it, beginning with the uncompleted Broken Pediment Tomb and the not very well named Renaissance Tomb, the small door of which sits rather awkwardly under a raised segmental pediment. Higher up a generous flight of steps mounts to a subsidiary wadi and the complex of the Roman Soldier Tomb, the porticoed courtyard of which, built rather than hewn from the rock, has been partly excavated. The tomb is on the right, the façade with four pilasters supporting a pediment, the chamber with recesses, and a smaller room to the left. On the left is the most elaborate of Nabataean triclinia. Externally there is nothing apart from openings in the rock. But within, the walls are flanked by fluted pilasters divided by niches and supporting a cornice. Here the colours of the rock are almost lurid, a tired red and a near purple that are only emphasized by the greyish veins of the sandstone.

Beyond the courtyard what is arguably the most beautiful of Nabataean stairs rises to a wider opening between the cliffs. On the left, facing this natural court, is the elegant Garden Triclinium, with a portico in antis. Beside this is the dam of a reservoir that still holds back enough water to sustain a substantial tree. The route continues up what is in effect a natural ramp, at the top of which steps lead up to the left. The ascent is

Steps to the High Place.

steep, with flights of steps punctuated by more level sections. The way circles up towards the now headless Lion Fountain, the water for which was channelled down the cliff: a narrow stair in the rock made it possible to control the flow. A little further on the path cuts through the rock; below, on the left, an outcrop overhangs a small sanctuary, with a relief representing Dushara. Look down to the Roman Soldier's Tomb.

The path approaches the High Place from the south. On the right are the two obelisks that were created when the summit of the hill to which these gave its name, Zibb 'Attuf ('merciful phallus'), was quarried away. Ahead, across a gully, the path circles up round the precariously balanced wall of a fort, which has been attributed to the Nabataeans but may possibly be of Crusader build, to the High Place. The name is apt. Here, high on the top of the jebel, and overlooking much of the city, the Nabataeans came to make their sacrifices and must have sensed the proximity of their gods. The rock was cut away to create a rectangular space with walls no more than a few inches high and a small raised 'table' for offerings, almost, but not quite, aligned on the raised altar on a low free-standing platform to the left: four steps to the left of the latter are associable with the shallow circular basin in two levels cut into the rock near by: this was used both for purification before ceremonies and for washing after sacrifices had been made, and was evidently supplied from the small tank south of the High Place. The ground falls away to the north. Here too the Nabataeans left their trace.

The High Place should ideally be visited as early in the day as possible, and before there is too much company. The façade of the Deir is in shadow until the sun has worked its way round to the south, and it is understandable that so many people wish to walk to it in the later afternoon. The route strikes northwards from the museum up a wadi. Soon after the steps begin there is a minor wadi on the left, at the head

The Obelisk.

of which is the eroded but not uninteresting Lion Triclinium. Return to the steps and continue upwards. Some way up the first subsidiary wadi on the right there is a good biclinium, adorned with urns but little visited. The valley floor opens out, but then the Nabataean stair continues, twisting and turning on the ascent, passing to the right of the Hermitage, a group of four caves marked with crosses, before finally reaching a high partly artificial plateau just to the south of the massive temple, the Deir ('monastery'), from which the plateau takes its name.

The Deir is cut back into the cliff, its scale – 40.2 by 46.9 metres/132 by 154 feet – only emphasized by the simplicity of the design, which is in two tiers, with above the gaping portal – itself 8 metres/26 feet high – a tholos surmounted by a huge urn and flanked by a broken pediment on paired pilasters. Steps to the left, not always accessible, give access to the top of the monument, and I still feel slightly sickened to recall a Bedouin youth who was leaping on to and off the urn on my first visit. The Deir was originally approached through a porticoed forecourt. Opposite the Deir, cut into an eroded outcrop, is an unusually large chamber with a finely carved niche. From the higher ground near this one can make out the line of the large stone circle (or more accurately oval) to the north-west of the Deir.

The plateau narrows as it rises to the north-west. There are numerous other cuttings in the cliff to the east, including a relief of two men with camels, in a small gorge some 68 metres/75 yards from the Deir. To the west there are low outcrops, beyond which the hills fall away dramatically. At the north end of the plateau there is a final outcrop. A path to the left of this circles round to a lower protuberance, which seems to hang above the jagged cliffs. There is a cistern, the displaced iron covering of which implies recent use, and beyond this a modest High Place, lined with low 'benches'. Loitering here, savouring what Berenson might have termed the tonic light that suffuses the spines of the ridges falling away to the Wadi Araba, it is impossible to believe that the Nabataeans were indifferent to their landscape. Linger if you can, but take care on the downward path when dusk falls, and savour the magic of the siq at night.

Petra deserves all the time you can lavish on it. One never tires of the siq, but nonetheless it is rewarding to take the three other routes that lead to the city from Wadi Musa: that through Wadi Shi'b Qays, which begins to the north the Rest House and passes below the fragment of an ancient aquaduct; the Wadi Mudhlim route, from the entrance to the siq, through the Nabataean tunnel; and the path up from the Bab as-Siq to Al Madras, with a number of ingenious water systems and shrines, and on across a plateau to descend to the Treasury or cross to the High Place. And do not miss Al Wu'eira, Le Vaux Moise ('valley of Moses') of the Crusaders, which is easily reached from the road to Bdul. The castle, built in 1116 when the Crusaders sought to secure control of their Oultrejourdain, was lost in 1144, only to be recovered, before falling to Saladin in 1188. It was defended from the east by a deep gully, which is crossed by a rock-cut bridge and gatehouse. The ruins of the roughly rectangular enceinte are much eroded – there is fallen masonry in every gully – and even the best-preserved towers in the west wall and at the north-east corner are fragmentary. But the prospect westwards across the equally eroded hills is memorable and, particularly at dusk, there is something strangely compelling about the evidence of earlier Nabataean exploitation of the site: stairs that now lead nowhere climbing exposed outcrops, rooms gouged from the rock and a house which the Crusaders adapted as an observation post. What must they have thought of the strange ruins among which they found themselves, and which after they were driven from their Oultrejourdain would not be seen by any European for over six hundred years? As one ponders on such matters, Al Wu'eira seems a proper place from which to take leave of Petra.

44. SIQ AL-BARID and BEIDHA

Petra, as a capital and a major entrepôt, did not exist in isolation. Some 6 kilometres/3¾ miles to the north, and 8 kilometres/5 miles by the road from Wadi Musa that passes Al-Wu'eira, there was a substantial settlement. The size of this is suggested by the numerous channels in the cliffs and cisterns that caught the water which the Nabataeans needed both for themselves and for their fields. A narrow break in the cliffs opens to the Siq Al-Barid, advertised by tour guides as 'Little Petra'. On the north side, cut well back into the cliff and thus relatively well protected from the wind, is the elegant pedimented façade of a temple with angle pilasters, the doorcase with a segmental pediment reached from a narrow court above a wide flight of steps.

Beyond this a wall controlled access to the siq, a gorge extending westwards for just 0.4 kilometres/under ¼ mile, opening out into three wider sections. In the first of these, on the left, above a house cut into the rock, is the beautiful temple with a portico in antis, the freestanding central columns of which have been reinstated. Across the siq there is a deep cistern. The gorge narrows to open out again, with a sequence of three triclinia, the matching façades of which are pilastered, on the north. The siq's name in Arabic, meaning the 'cool gorge', is apt, for it was partly sheltered from the sun, and so one can well imagine those who lived or transacted business taking refuge in the triclinia during the remorseless summer days. Opposite there is an even bigger triclinium. Beyond this is the most precious survival of Al-Barid, the Painted House of the first century AD, approached up a modern stair. The main room is a biclinium, the back wall of which retains much of the original plastered decoration of *trompe l'oeil* masonry with courses of white blocks and red pointing in two layers. Off this, sensibly protected by a screen, is a chamber with two niches on the back wall and single ones at either side. The ceiling, which has been responsibly restored, is painted with a field of vines: birds peck at bunches of grapes while *amorini* and a satyr disport. This type of decoration was popular in antiquity, and was to be revived in the Renaissance by no less an artist than Leonardo, who, however, dispensed with the diminutive figures in his tragically repainted ceiling in Milan.

Throughout the siq there are flights of steps. A fine example is in the third and final opening. Behind a small tree on the right a long stair rises to a small open-air biclinium, below a small dam in two sections on either side of an isolated rock that caught the water ingeniously channelled from the rock above. On my last visit I lingered here, while two Bedouin women coaxed their flock through the gorge, and up the narrow cleft at the end, where over seventy-five Nabataean steps are still more or less serviceable after two millennia's use. The stair emerges on a shelf with views that make one wish for time to follow the ancient routes beyond, whether to Petra or down to the Wadi Araba.

Return to the entrance to the siq and follow the cliff round to the right, for a ten-minute walk to the Neolithic village of Beidha, or Seyl Aqlat, which was discovered by Miss Diana Kirkbride in 1956. This was occupied from about 7000 BC for some 500 years and developed in eight phases. The site stands forward from the northern flank of a wide valley, above lower ground to the south, on a rise falling away on the west to the bed of the wadi, the erosion of which has destroyed part of the village. Despite this the ruins, although not visually spectacular, are readily intelligible to the non-specialist. There are clusters of round structures, set into the ground: the roofs were supported on timber posts, which of course have gone, leaving vertical gaps in the stone walls that were built round them. The village was walled, as is seen most easily at the south-east, where a flight of five steps survives from an entrance. To the east there was a shrine, not far from a group of reconstructions of characteristic houses that may help some visitors to visualize the Neolithic village.

Querns.

More eloquent than these to me are the many querns scattered round the site, irregular stones averaging 60 centimetres/24 inches across which have been carefully hollowed out. It was in these that were ground the barley and wheat cultivated by this early agricultural community.

45. WADI SABRA

Al-Barid's southern counterpart was at Sabra in the wadi of that name, the walk to which is one of the great pleasures of visiting Petra. The route cuts to the south of the Colonnaded Street, passing below the splendid group of tombs on the flank of Umm al-Biyara, and then striking upwards on the path below the eyrie Snake Monument. This represents a coiled serpent, symbolizing immortality, on a squared pedestal. On the more level ground beyond, just after a house where tea is served, a track to the right leads to the Jebel Haroun, the tomb of Aaron, the shrine on which is clearly caught in the morning light as a spec of brilliant white on the distant summit. In 1812 Burckhardt persuaded his guide that he was pledged to sacrifice there and thus was able to have his furtive view of the forgotten ruins of Petra. The track to Sabra continues southwards, curling down to the left to pass the Birkat ad-Darb, an impressive wayside cistern. Rainwater was channelled from the rocks, and fed through two filtering pools to the large underground reservoir, to which steps in three flights descend.

A little further on, a crest is reached, and the path begins to drop gradually into a valley that eventually debouches into the Wadi Sabra: on the descent the light catches the retaining wall of the ancient road, zigzagging on its way. The occasional herdsman or woman apart, no human is in sight. And on my first visit, five days after heavy rain, only one other set of footsteps defiled the smooth sandy bed of the stream which had already run dry. But of course there were sounds: the bells of sheep and goats, a cow high up somewhere, birds, the scuttling of a lizard.

The most conspicuous monument of Sabra is the small but elegant Roman theatre, built against the foot of the eastern cliff and partly rock cut. The rows of benches are preserved at the south end. The seats of the upper row, evidently favoured by the local cognoscenti, were supplied with backs. Above the theatre is the retaining wall of a reservoir, which was fed by channels from above, and made it possible to fill the orchestra with water. De Laborde, who was for the most part unimpressed by the calibre of what he saw at Sabra, was evidently fascinated by the thought that *naumachiae* (mock naval battles) were performed in so unlikely a spot. Alas, the columns he saw, faced in plaster and with traces of a deep red paint, have gone. And now the fragmentary walls in the valley floor opposite, which have been thought to represent a barracks, are being eaten away by the winter floods. It is clear that Sabra was a flourishing satellite of Petra, a staging post perhaps for merchants, but one that must also have served as a base for the mining industry, as the area is rich in copper. Moreover, water from the spring of 'Ain Sabra, south of the theatre, meant that part at least of the valley could be cultivated by the Nabataeans. On the way back one notices more: a small area quarried in the rock, hints of walls.

The theatre.

46. HUMAYMA

Driving down the escarpment of the Ras an-Naqab to the sand-strewn Hisma at its feet, it is difficult to believe that a significant city could have survived in so ill favoured a terrain for nigh on a millennium. Yet such was indeed the case. As the Byzantine historian Uranius recorded, the Nabataean king Obodas I was told to search for a place called Auara, which means white in both Nabataean and Arabic, and his son, Aretas III (87–62 BC), saw a man in white on a camel of the same colour, and thus knew where he was to establish the town. Only the brilliance of his people at managing water made the project possible, and the town – Hawara to the Nabataeans, Havarra to the Romans and Byzantines, and Humayma in the early Islamic period – became a significant staging post on the route from Petra to Aqaba, and later on the Via Nova Traiana, its fort manned by a local cavalry regiment, the Equites Sagitarii Indigenae. As the identification of five churches indicates, the place continued to prosper under the Byzantines. But it was in the eighth century that Humayma witnessed the preparations for one of the turning points of Islamic history. Kinsmen of the Prophet by descent from his uncle al-Abbas, the Abbasids, had settled there, building a qasr very much on the lines of those of the Umayyads, whose caliphate they were destined to destroy.

The site is now posted from the main road, and indeed boasts a visitor centre. This looks rather forlorn, but is conveniently placed. To the north is the Roman fort, which may be of Trajan's time, and thus more or less contemporary with the imperial annexation of the Nabataean kingdom. The fort is aligned north to south, the north-west corner lying close to the remarkable Nabataean aqueduct, a covered channel that drew on three springs some 20 kilometres/12½ miles to the north, which supplied the fine reservoir with rounded corners just within the walls. Part of the east wall, including the gate, has been excavated, as have a number of not particularly impressive buildings within the fort.

To the west of the south-west corner of the fort is a substantial Nabataean reservoir, also fed from the aqueduct, and with an outflow. Further south is a small bath complex of seven rooms. The furnace was walled in brick; other rooms have benches, and in two there are flues connecting with the hypocausts below. The building overlay an earlier Nabataean one and indeed one of the fascinating things about Humayma is the way in which its layers accumulated. As the Via Nova Traiana was aligned on the earlier aqueduct, so Roman and subsequent buildings in what was evidently the heart of the town took advantage of the facilities the Nabataeans had created. There are numerous cisterns, but none is more splendid than that beside a huge pile of excavators' spoil.

The restored cistern.

Originally covered – only two of the arches on which the roof was borne are in place – this has been cemented for reuse, as have the channel and filtering tank, as well as the outflow. Near by is a similar cistern, not fully cleared, fourteen of the roofing arches of which are in place.

Of the five churches that have been identified at Humayma, the most obviously impressive is the so-called Lower Church, some 200 metres/218 yards south-west of the two cisterns. This was of basilica type, with a raised chancel and benches along the back and lateral walls. Some of the paving is in place, and to judge from the quality of two marble panels from this, now in the museum at Aqaba, the church was of considerable distinction.

Another of the churches in the town, just to the north of the cisterns, was taken over by the builders of an early Islamic structure. But it seems, if the attribution to them of the qasr south of the visitor centre is valid, that the Abbasids preferred to build from scratch. The qasr had a recessed entrance on the east, which opened to a central courtyard, off which the necessary domestic rooms were laid out: the most remarkable finds made by the excavators from the University of Victoria are a group of ivory fittings, now also at Aqaba. The qasr was clearly the centre of a significant agricultural enterprise, for it is known that the Abbasids planted 500 olive trees. Nonetheless, for them to gravitate from a life of comfortable obscurity, admittedly in a place close to the main Haj pilgrimage route, to ruling most of the Muslim world from Baghdad was a remarkable achievement.

47. WADI RUM

Wadi Rum is by any standard spectacular. The striking silhouette of the mountains comes into sight on the descent towards Humayma, but it is only on the approach that one sees that the wadi was literally a natural gateway to the great stretch of desert to the south through which trade must have passed since time immemorial. The level sandy floor of the wadi, hardly a kilometre/half a mile wide at its narrowest point, lies between two ranges of the Shara mountains, the Jebel umm Ashreen on the east and the Jebel Rum opposite, the sheer flanks of which rise up to 800 metres/2,600 feet. Early man was, of course, drawn to Rum not for the drama of the landscape but because water was available from a few springs that ooze in some places where the sandstone of the mountains rests on the underlying granite. Many of the small structures in the wadi have thus far defied accurate dating, but it is clear that some of them antedate the Nabataeans. They in their turn were followed by the Thamudic peoples. Thereafter Rum sinks from Western view. For an Anglo-Saxon audience at least, the place is inevitably associated with T. E. Lawrence, who chose it as a base in 1917 during the Arab Revolt and described it so memorably in the *Seven Pillars of Wisdom*. Rum is now a major tourist destination.

Mass tourism comes at a price: in the case of Rum this is signalled by the new visitor centre, some 7 kilometres/4½ miles north of the village. Armed with an appropriately expensive ticket, one can then drive on to near the old resthouse beside the village that has grown up round the toy-like fort of the Arab Legion. In the twenty years that I have known this, the settlement has expanded southwards; and although it is understandable that local families have to be accommodated, this expansion has inevitably affected some of the fragile antiquities in the area. The car park too has

grown. A short way to the west of this, mercifully concealed from view by a low ridge and just below the cliff face, is what survives of the lower courses of the Nabataeans' temple, dedicated to Allat, a goddess of the Arabs who may have been the consort of Dushara. Steps from the east led through a portico in antis to the central hall of the cella, the walls of which, originally decorated with paint, were lined with engaged columns that were fluted with plaster. In the centre there was a free-standing shrine. Behind the hall were further rooms, and at the corners on the west side stairs up to the roof, which had so important a role in both Nabataean and Syrian cults. Graffiti in the script of the Thamudic tribes – Arabs first mentioned in 716 BC who subsequently became allies of Rome – show that they adopted the temple when the Nabataeans were eclipsed. Behind the temple are the eroded walls of a villa with a thermal complex, the builder of which must surely have had a close connection with the temple.

Left: The Naba-
taean temple.
Far left: Wadi um
Ishrin.

South of the temple, across what is in effect a sandy bay cut into the jebel, is the path up to 'Ain ash-Shallaleh ('the spring of the waterfall'), water from which, once channelled by the Nabataeans to a cistern, is now piped to the village. Allat was invoked here too and there are numerous Nabataean cuttings. Modern concrete may disappoint those whose expectations have been aroused by Lawrence's description of the place. From here, if time allows, walk on, passing the village. A mile or so further on, on the far side of a bastion of the mountain, is a second well, Ain Aina, below which there is usually a Bedouin encampment: the short scramble is worthwhile both for the scent of the *hadek* (a lemon verbena, used locally for an infusion) and for the view over the southern approach to the wadi.

More appealing than the Nabataean temple are the lesser archaeological remains in which Wadi Rum and the area abounds: the Thamudic names found on so many prominent rocks, often in association with schematic scratchings of men and animals; the roughly paved enclosures, edged

with stones and with near the back – or in the back wall – one or three rather larger standing blocks, which are laid out singly or in small clusters below the cliffs on both sides of the valley; and the small circles of white stones set in the sand in the centre of the wadi at either end, modest counterparts of that beside the Deir at Petra which, as I know from personal experience, can be rather difficult to find. These in particular must be vulnerable to the increasing number of four-wheel-drive vehicles that pound across the sands, heading out to the Bedouin encampments that take in tourists and the ranges beyond. None of the tours on offer should disappoint; but those with a taste for Thamudic inscriptions, even if like me they cannot read them, should aim to visit the remarkable canyon at the north end of the Jebel Khazali, the mountain that dominates the southern approaches to Rum, some 3 kilometres/2 miles across the sand.

The authorities have done their best to protect Rum. And we, the tourists, must do ours to respect the place, and then savour our memories of it, of the sights and also of the sounds: the muezzin's call reverberating from the concave cliff of Jebel umm Ashreen; the sounds that break the silence of the valley at night, as the bark of a dog is taken up by another, and echoed by the camels who in turn protest at the passing of a vehicle. Once a place of passage, Rum is now an outpost of the Bedouin way of life.

Stone circle.

48. AQABA

Aqaba is not the most prepossessing of the cities of Jordan. But as the country's only port it makes a crucial contribution to the kingdom's economy. In a sense there is nothing new in this. King Solomon had a port in Edomite territory on the Red Sea, which can only have been on what is now the Gulf of Aqaba. The Nabataeans cannot have been unaware of the area's potential; and when Trajan took over their kingdom in AD 106 he projected the Via Nova Traiana from Bosra to Aqaba as the backbone of the defence of the Empire's new territory. But there is little to show for the Roman Ailana or for Byzantine Ayla, two capitals in the museum apart. The Islamic town of Ayla, set to the east of its predecessor, was occupied from the seventh century until the tenth. The Crusaders took Aqaba in 1116, building a castle of which nothing now survives, but lost this to Saladin in 1171. The early sixteenth-century Mameluke fortress that survives may have replaced a late medieval outpost, and was in turn altered under the Ottomans. To them it was of particular importance in connection with the Haj. The Ottomans' eventual loss of Aqaba in 1917 to the Sherif of Mecca and his allies is graphically described by T. E. Lawrence.

The dusty remains of Ayla, overlooked by a housing development, are off the main coastal road near the centre of the town. Appropriately the most conspicuous building is the mosque, which had a double colonnade to the east and a single one on the west. The walls, surviving sections of which have been consolidated, were laid out with rounded towers, but merit no more than a brief glance.

Further south are the Mameluke fort and, below this, the museum, both

The gatehouse to the Mameluke fort.

of which are much more rewarding. In the forecourt of the latter are four Roman milestones, while a fifth, from Khirbet al-Khaldi, the penultimate fort in the sequence on the Via Nova Traiana on the approach to Aqaba, is in the museum itself. Near by are two Byzantine capitals, representing Saints Longinus and Theodore, and in a style surprisingly close to some Romanesque sculpture in the West. In the same room is a beautiful fragment of Fatimid pottery, with the head of a turbaned man.

But it is the finds from Humayma that impress most. There is characteristic Nabataean pottery, including a small bowl with what was evidently a popular palmette pattern. There are two white marble decorative panels from the Lower Church. And most remarkable of all, the group of ivory fittings found in the Abbasid qasr. There are narrow borders with vine and bird motifs, and, most remarkably, a panel of a soldier in profile to the left, wearing a helmet of chain mail and with his sword at his side. One cannot help wondering if the carver or his patron had known some very much earlier Mesopotamian relief; and certainly the man from Humayma, with his strong nose, would not have been out of place in Assyria.

49. PUNON: KHIRBET FEINAN

Feinan deserves to be better known. The ruins of the town, which in antiquity was known as Phaeno and probably represents Punon, where Moses pitched his tents on his way from Egypt, tumble over a ridge between the wadis Dana and Salawan, both usually dry, which meet as the Wadi Feinan just to the west. The ranges of sandstone hills stretching down towards the Wadi Araba were riddled with deposits of copper, which was mined in the area as early as 4000 BC. The Edomites owed their wealth to the industry, and this was maintained with vigour by the Romans and their Byzantine successors. Christians were sentenced to slavery in the mines at Phaeno during Diocletian's persecutions, and in their turn the Byzantines sent those they regarded as religious deviants to penal servitude there. Thereafter Phaeno was forgotten, except in the hagiography of the saints who died there, including the Egyptian bishop Peleus, who was stoned to death. It was rediscovered by the Austrian Alois Musil, author of *Arabia Petraea* (Vienna, 1907), and visited, with some difficulty, by Louis Goldring, whose *In the Steps of Moses the Conqueror* (London, 1938) gives an almost lurid impression of the place.

Feinan is indeed an astonishing site. The energetic can walk down the wadi from Dana, but an easier approach is from a turn to Qurayqira (pronounced 'graygra') off the main road down the Wadi Araba. The metalled road ends among houses just beyond the reception centre for the Feynan Ecolodge, which is unquestionably the most convenient centre from which to visit not only Feinan itself but also Umm al-Amad and Nahas. The rough track continues up the wide valley. On the approach to the town there are parallel fields, most easily made out in the morning when the low terraces are seen in shadow. The track crosses the dry stream bed and passes a large complex, evidently a monastery, which lies just below the ridge across which the ruin bed sprawls. On the western slope among the heaped piles of masonry is what survives of the apse of a church. Above there are crumbled walls, mostly of roughly hewn masonry, for Phaeno had no aspiration to refinement. It is only as one progresses along the crest that the size of the town fully registers.

Among the fallen stones and the mounds of shapeless slag, the sharp light catches the sheen of once molten surfaces, congealed since antiquity to resemble fragments of broken relief maps in black. The sides of the ridge are pockmarked with such piles of slag. So is the higher ground east of the town. Others blacken much of the level area to the north.

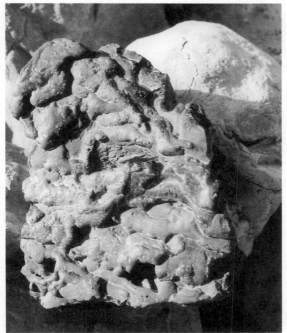

Left: slag.
Right: the aqueduct.

Yet more are ranged along the lower ridge across the Wadi Salawan to the south, from the point where a subsidiary wadi, the Ash Sheger, runs into it. Water from the tangled mountains beyond was brought in a channel lined with small rounded stones set in concrete to an aqueduct, of which one arch and the stumps of the next two piers survive on the east side of the Wadi Ash Sheger, protected by their position from the full impact of the flash floods that have long since eaten away their erstwhile companions. From the west bank, where the walls of a camping site are an unfortunate intrusion since my first visit, the channel ran westwards, passing the slag heaps, black against the sandy soil, to the deep filtering tank of an impressive reservoir, some 33 metres/36 yards square, lined with regular masonry of which twelve courses are visible. At the north-west corner there is a flight of steps, near which an outflow drained surplus water to a further channel that ends, where the ground falls away, in a mill, much of the structure of which is in place. Naturally the water from the mill was too precious to waste: this was used in long parallel fields below, the low terraced walls of which have already been mentioned.

The visitor to Feinan will want to see at least one token mine. The simplest course is to follow a track north of the town that crosses the valley floor to a low ridge above the Wadi Khalid. Walk up the stream bed, which descends from the north-east. Some way up there is a substantial slag heap above the bank on the left: at the back of this is a square vertical shaft, off which there is a horizontal passage. A little further on, to the right, the rock is veined in green. Just beyond is the rough-hewn entrance to a horizontal shaft, perhaps 12.25 metres/40 feet deep. In places one can stand, but more often it is necessary to crawl. Even allowing for the debris of two millennia it is obvious that the men who worked in such places knew very cramped conditions.

Endeavours to protect historic sites and ecology do not always benefit the local people. But those responsible for the Dana Nature Reserve understand the interests of the Azazmeh, the Bedouin of the area. On my first visit there was only too much evidence of illicit digging: now the ruins are protected. And those who stay at Feinan can linger in the twilight, as the hills are suffused with pink, and the sounds of excited children rise from the Bedouin camps. But these too are children of a changing world. Walking back in the dusk, I noticed a pretty girl, of ten or twelve perhaps, sitting by the wayside.

'Stop.' A loud command!

I did.

'Where are you from?'

'England.'

'What is your name?'

'Francis. What is your name?'

'Ayesha.'

She was perhaps too young to have reached the age of inhibition, but spoke with what was to me an unexpected freedom.

50. UMM AL-AMAD

Umm al-Amad is one of the most haunting sites in Jordan. And even now it requires some effort, and indeed expenditure, to get there. The most sensible course is to stay at the Feynan Ecolodge, which will arrange for a driver to take you to the nearest practical point from which to set out on what is a moderately strenuous walk, and supply a guide. The road from the village crosses a level stony wadi, with a scattering of acacia trees, and then turns to a narrower valley where in the winter some Bedouin families are encamped. The going gets rougher, and soon the walk begins. I was lucky to have a guide, Armad Gawasmeh, who understood instinctively what I wanted to be told.

Some way below the cave Armad picked up a small shard. The chain of hills ahead, silhouetted against the morning sky, grew more rather than less intimidating. We walked up to a smooth knob and then cut upwards, moving carefully among fallen stones. Except at one point where a cut perhaps a yard deep had been made across a spine of rock for a path that crossed ours, there were none of the usual signs that we were on an ancient route. Further on we looked down on a juniper in a cleft, but higher up we passed the skeletons of others, whose valiant roots had been defeated by recent droughts. We gained a ridge and made over high ground, with striking views, before reaching a further crest, where we paused to look down into an enclosed valley, enchained by cliffs, that falls away to a jagged canyon. Armad pointed to Umm al-Amad, squat cuttings in the rock on a steep slope between the cliffs that rise more or less to the summit of the mountain behind and a line of rock that hangs above the ravine.

There are three main openings, originally perhaps 1.25 metres/4 feet high: to the left are two smaller ones, while on the right the rock is partly undercut. The name Umm al-Amad means 'mother of the columns'. The description is accurate. One moves in to see a succession of columns, not tall classical ones but stubby squat piers, the concave outlines of which are eloquent of the weight these bear. Near the linked entrances the walls have been blackened by the smoke of Bedouin fires, but as one progresses the rock is uniformly brown, except where at intervals of roughly 20 centimetres/8 inches it has been scored by the miners' implements. The columns are roughly aligned. Ahead there are six rows, but to the right there are as many as eight, a few cut almost square. Even from the remotest recesses one can often see some glimmer of the natural light and at least one concave wall seems almost to have had the function of reflecting this, but cuttings in the walls imply that whoever worked on them did so by the light of lanterns. Near the back a raised platform has been left uncut.

Umm al-Amad.

Although there are a few green pebbles near by, there is no obvious sign of the presence of copper in the bedrock, and no evidence whatever of this being processed near by, as one sees at the many mines of the area. But what other purpose could the complex have served? Is it conceivable that people planned to take refuge in so inaccessible and waterless a place? And how clear is it that the Romans were involved? I sat and pondered, drinking Armad's tea and gazing at the cliffs opposite. We heard a bird, whose call was unfamiliar. Armad turned to a page in his book and passed it to me: the bird was a brown-necked raven, which we saw later with its mate. Otherwise we had the place to ourselves. Eventually we left. Some way below the caves Armad picked up a piece of coarse pottery that I would not have noticed in the dust. 'Old,' I asserted. 'Iron Age, maybe Bronze Age,' he rejoined, adding: 'Anyway, it's a long time ago.' Later, I hung back and, when about to catch up, realized that Armad had by some instinct that the Nabateans would have readily understood found a high place of his own from which to direct his prayers to Mecca.

51. KHIRBET AN-NAHAS

Khirbet an-Nahas is hardly 8 kilometres/5 miles as the crow flies to the north-west of Feinan on the further side of a spine of hills descending towards the Wadi Araba. Even now it takes a measure of determination to get to the 'copper ruin', as the name means in Arabic. A track runs north from Gurayqira, passing to the west of 'Ain al-Fidan, a perpetual spring of considerable local importance. Just beyond a promontory on which an early site has recently been excavated, the route crosses the rocky stream bed of the Wadi Fidan and climbs over open country with wide views towards a shoulder before descending to the level floor of the Wadi Gruwebe. Even in a four-wheel-drive vehicle the going is slow, the sand unpredictable. A single herdsman has the entire valley to himself and his flock. To the east the hills close in at either side. Nahas spreads over a low shelf south of the valley on the west side of a subsidiary wadi.

There is a bleak beauty about the place in winter; and even then the wadis are almost invariably waterless. The copper-bearing sandstone hills of the area have been exploited since Bronze Age times, and much of what can be seen at Nahas dates from the Iron Age, when the smelting industry was vital to the economy of the Edomites. The Nabataeans and the Romans followed in their turn. Just above the wadi is a walled camp, roughly 73 metres/80 yards square, with a substantial tower at the centre of the north-west side. Other structures both within the enclosure and outside it have been excavated. There is no finesse about these. They were built for a single purpose, to extract copper from the local stone. Around them are heaped drifts of the slag that was discharged from the furnaces, congealing as it cooled, the once liquid surfaces now shining in the sunlight. This industrial waste is spread along the bank of the side wadi and stretches for some distance to the south and west of the camp.

Slag heaps and fallen buildings.

Although there is a spring in the area, and the wadis must have flowed after rain, the lack of water must have been an almost insuperable problem at Nahas. There is no evidence of any sophisticated water catchment system, let alone of an aqueduct as at Feinan. So it has been suggested that Nahas was used only intermittently, when water was available. We will no doubt know more when the reports of the Canadian team that has discovered and consolidated so much at Nahas have been fully published. But even without the forensic information the archaeologists will bring to bear, we can well imagine the travails of those who were put to work in so inhospitable a terrain.

The square enclosure has been interpreted as a concentration camp, and thus as a predecessor of those in which the Romans confined the workforces they needed to extract the precious porphyry of Mons

The camp.

Porphyrius in Eqypt or the prized yellow marble of Chemtou in Tunisia. And one's sense of wonder at the industry of the Edomites and their successors is tempered by a gnawing sense of unease.

52. DEIR' AIN' ABATA: THE CAVE OF LO

The Wadi Araba gradually falls away to the Dead Sea. Flanked by mountains on both sides, the harsh bare landscape changes as the valley becomes progressively more fertile. Man has long sought to tame this land, as, for example, in the ancient field system recorded near the Roman fort at Qasr et-Telah. Modern patterns of agriculture and the potash industry have imposed their character of the area, which with the land to the north as far as the Lisan Peninsula is known as the Southern Ghor, or depression. Whether approached from the south, or from the Wadi Karak, which descends through hillsides so drained of colour as to seem of another world, it seems hardly surprising to be told that the early 'cities of the plain', notably Sodom and Gomorrah and Zoar, were obliterated by the deity.

Zoar was the predecessor of unprepossessing Safi. And it was to Zoar that Lot fled with his wife and daughters, when told by the angel to leave Sodom. As they arrived, Lot's wife disobeyed the injunction not to look back on their city as it was destroyed by fire and was turned into a pillar of salt – not of course a substance of which there was a local shortage. Lot and his daughters installed themselves in a cave above the plain, and it was there, with the intention of securing posterity, that the girls tricked their drunken father into committing incest – ironically now generally considered a more serious matter than the sins for which Sodom and Gomorrah were destroyed – and thus into siring the founders of the Moabites and the Ammonites. The Byzantines, who well understood the potential of pilgrimage sites, recognized a small

The cistern.

cavern high above the valley as Lot's refuge. But even they would have been astonished by the scale of the new visitor centre.

A road from the centre twists up the wall of the valley to a car park. After a climb of 300 steps – for Lot was clearly thoroughly agile – the pilgrim arrives at the main door to a small courtyard that originally gave access to the small aisled basilica which the Byzantines constructed round the cave. This was built out from the hillside, and only part of the substructure of the narthex survives. The north aisle led to the cave itself, making it possible for pilgrims of differing religions to visit it without needing to enter the main section of the church. The floor of the aisle was decorated with a geometric mosaic. The cave was entered through a door in the middle of the lateral apse, the lintel of which is carved with a cross between stylized hexafoils: an inscription near by is dated 606. Small as it is, the cave proved on excavation to have been used from the Early Bronze Age onwards. The church was rebuilt in May 691, as an inscription establishes. The chancel is raised, and the apse is

surrounded by a synthronon, three rows of a bench for the clergy: there would originally have been an episcopal throne above this in the centre. Elements of the decorative scheme found during excavation are shown in the visitor centre.

The church did not, of course, exist in isolation. From the south aisle one can look down into a substantial double cistern, the roof of which was supported on arches. A channel on the west side of the further section directed water to the larger one by the church. The retaining wall needed to be supported by five substantial buttresses on the outward side. To the north are the remains of other buildings which formed part of the complex, including a refectory and, presumably, facilities for pilgrims to stay. The poor state of these structures, as of the church itself, is due to the steep angle of the slope on which they were constructed. Looking down on the ordered green rectangular fields at his feet, and out across the Southern Ghor towards the hills beyond the Dead Sea, the tourist of today can understand why a millennium and a half ago the Byzantines determined to commemorate the story of Lot, or Saint Lot as their dedicatory inscriptions assert, high on the flank of a stony hillside.

The church, with the door to the cave on the left.

GLOSSARY

Apsidal Of an apse.

Adyton Sanctuary within a temple.

Acropolis Fortress of a city or town.

Agora Square or marketplace.

Apodyterium Dressing room of a Roman bath.

Aramaic Language of the Aramaeans.

Bab Gate (Arabic).

Barrel vault Arched roof.

Basilica Type of Roman hall with lower side halls, which was used for many Byzantine churches.

Bayt Group of rooms round a central court (Arabic).

Bema Raised area in chancel of a Byzantine church.

Biclinium Room with two couches on which to recline.

Caldarium Hot room of a Roman bath.

Cardo maximus Main colonnaded street of a Roman town.

Cavea Auditorium of a theatre.

Cella Central chamber of a temple.

Chalcolithic Period between c.4500 and c.3200 BC.

Chert Rough desert with flint.

Corbel Block, or one of a series of blocks, supporting a beam.

Cyclopean Built of large blocks.

Decumanus Important cross street of a Roman town.

Decapolis Group of ten towns in northern Jordan and Syria.

Deir Monastery (Arabic).

Donjon Keep of a castle.

Exedra Semicircular recess.

Forum Marketplace.

Frigidarium Cold room of a Roman bath.

Glacis Sloping area, rock cut or built, below a defensive wall.

Haj Annual pilgrimage to Mecca.

Hammam Bath (Arabic).

Hexastyle Portico with six columns.

Hippodamian plan Town plan of a type devised by

Hippodamus of Miletus.

Iconoclasm Byzantine movement rejecting the representation of the human form.

Iwan Bay set within an open arch.

Jebel Mountain (Arabic).

Keep Inner stronghold of a castle.

Khan Caravansarai, warehouse-cum-hostel.

Loculus Recess in tomb for body.

Machicolation Projecting parapet with holes from which to attack assailants.

Minaret Tower of a mosque.

Mihrab Niche in mosque, usually aligned on Mecca.

Metope Gap in a Doric frieze between triglyphs.

Narthex Vestibule at the west end of a church.

Necropolis Cemetery.

Neolithic Period between c.6000 and c.4500 BC.

Notitia Dignitatum List of Roman commanders drawn up after 395.

Nymphaeum Fountain.

Odeon Small theatre.

Orchestra Semicircular space between the stage and auditorium of a theatre.

Paleolithic Period before c.20000 BC.

Palmette Plant motif, much used by the Nabataeans.

Peribolos Sacred enclosure.

Peristyle Covered colonnaded corridor round an internal courtyard, or outer colonnade of the cella of a peripteral temple.

Portico in antis Portico set back from the façade of a temple.

Praetorium Residence of a Roman governor, or barracks.

Principia Roman military headquarters.

Propylaeum Monumental entrance to a temenos.

Qalaat Castle (Arabic).

Qasr Palace (Arabic).

Rinceaux Scrolling ornament.

Saqiyah Wheel house (Arabic).

Siq Gorge (Arabic).

Squinch Arch set in the corner of a space to carry a dome.

Stele Upright stone, generally inscribed.

Strata Diocletiana Road from Sura on the Euphrates to Damascus.

Suq Market (Arabic).

Synthronon Bench for clergy in the apse of a Byzantine church.

Tell Mound built up by the debris of long-term occupation.

Temenos Sacred enclosure.

Tepidarium Warm room of a Roman bath.

Tetrapylon Four-sided structure at the intersection of major roads in a Roman city.

Tholos Circular building.

Triclinium Room with three couches, used for eating.

Vicus Civil settlement associated with a Roman fort.

Voussoir Shaped block used in the construction of an arch.

Wadi River or stream (Arabic).

PEOPLES AND DYNASTIES

Abbasids Rulers of Damascus from 750, who transferred their capital to Baghdad, founded in 762, and held the Caliphate until 968.

Ammonites People of the kingdom of Ammon, which emerged after 1200 BC between the Wadi Mujib and the river Zarqa.

Assyrians Mesopotamian state that dominated Syria, including Jordan, from 856 to 612 BC.

Ayyubids Dynasty founded by Saladin, which controlled Syria, including Jordan, from 1176 until 1260.

Byzantines Successors to the empire transferred in AD 330 from Rome to Byzantium, later renamed Constantinople, which controlled Syria, including Jordan, until 636.

Circassians Refugees from Circassia, displaced by the Russians.

Crusaders Christians who sought to recover the Holy Places and defend these, occupying much of what is now Jordan in 1115, but losing this after the Battle of Hattin in 1187.

Druzes Adherents of a religious sect founded by the Fatimid Al-Hakim (996–1021), long settled in the Lebanon, many of whom migrated to the Hauran in the nineteenth century and subsequently settled at Azraq and elsewhere in Jordan.

Edomites People of the kingdom of Edom, which emerged after 1200 BC, south of the Wadi Hasa.

Franks Crusaders.

Gadarenes People of Gadara.

Hasmonaeans Jewish dynasty founded by John Hyrcanus, which gained control of Judea after the death of the Seleucid Antiochus VII in 129 BC.

Hellenistic Phase of Greek rule in Syria, including Jordan, that began with Alexander's victory at Issus in 333 BC and endured until the collapse of Seleucid power after 164 BC.

Mamelukes A military oligarchy that held power in Cairo and controlled Syria, including Jordan, from 1260 until the Ottoman conquest of 1516.

Moabites People of the kingdom of Moab, between the Wadis Mujib and Hasa, who emerged in the Early Iron Age.

Mongols Central Asian tribes united by Genghis Khan, whose successors invaded parts of the Near East in devastating waves between 1260 and 1401.

Nabataeans Arabs whose control of trade routes to the south allowed them to build up a substantial position east of Jordan, which passed to Roman control after the death of King Rabbel II in AD 106.

Ottomans Turkish dynasty, with capitals successively at Bursa, Edirne and from 1453 Istanbul, which added Syria, including Jordan, to its empire in 1516, was at its zenith under Suleiman the Magnificent (1520–66) and held the area until 1918.

Ptolemies Dynasty founded by Ptolemy, which ruled Egypt after the death of Alexander the Great (323 BC).

Sasanians Rulers of Persia from AD 224, who in turn challenged Roman and Byzantine control of the Near East.

Seleucids Dynasty founded by Seleucus I Nicator (311–281 BC), which ruled Syria and much of the Near East from Antioch.

Thamudic tribes Federation of tribes, which had been settled in Arabia by 716 BC and became allied of Rome after AD 106.

Umayyads Dynasty of caliphs established by Moawiya (661–81) at Damascus, which controlled the Near East until 750.

CHRONOLOGY

BC

c.3300–2250	Early Bronze Age.
c.2250–1550	Middle Bronze Age.
c.1550–1200	Late Bronze Age.
c.1200–539	Iron Age: emergence of kingdoms of Ammon, Moab and Edom.
	Assyrian domination.
539–333	Persian control.
333	Defeat at Issus of Darius II by Alexander the Great (336–323).
198	Conquest of southern Syria by Antiochus III (223–187).
c.168	Aretas I, Nabataean king.
86–62	Reign of Aretas III.
64	Conquest of Syria by Pompey.
4	Death of Herod the Great.

AD

106	The annexation of the Nabatean kingdom by the Emperor Trajan (98–117) and creation of the province of Arabia.
	The reign of the Emperor Hadrian.
	The reign of the Emperor Constantine.
395	The division of the Roman Empire.
573	Syria raided by Chosroes I.
606	The conquest of Syria by Chosroes II.
629	Byzantine victory over the Muslims at Mota.

636	Muslim victory over the Byzantines at the Battle of the Yarmuk.
661–750	Umayyad period.
750–968	Abbasid period.
969–1055	Fatimid period.
1055–1128	Seljuk period.
1097–1102	The First Crusade.
1099	The conquest of Jerusalem by the Crusaders.
1115	Montreal (Shobak) founded by King Baldwin I.
1128–74	Zengid period.
1146–1260	Ayyubid period
1176-9	Reign of Saladin.
1187	Saladin's victory over the Crusaders at Hattin.
1187-92	The Third Crusade.
1260	Defeat of the Mongols by the Mamelukes at Ain Julad.
1260-1516	Mameluke Period.
1260-77	Reign of Sultan Baibars.
1517	Ottoman conquest of Syria.
1914-18	First World War.
1916	Beginning of the Arab Revolt.
1921	Abdullah Emir of Trans-Jordan, under the British Mandate.
1946	Jordan declared a kingdom, under Abdullah.
1948	Withdrawal of British from Palestine and Jordan.
1953-99	Reign of King Hussein.
1967	Six Day War.
1999	Accession of King Abdullah

INDEX

Page numbers in *italic* refer to
illustrations

A

Abbasids 8, 15, 186, 188
Abdullah, King 9, 10, 14, 25, 26
Abila 55–9
  basilica 56, *57*, 58
  painted tombs 58
  theatre 56
Aeropolis 122
'Ain as-Sil 80
'Ain Ghazel 14, 20
Al-Habis 52–4, *53*
Al-Qanatir 113–14
Al-Qasr 121–2, *121*
Al-Qastal 98–100, *99*
Al-Qatrana 132–3, *132*
Al-Wu'eira 13, 179
Al'Aina 141
Alexander the Great 15, 42
Alexander Jannaeus 42, 46, 109
Amman 14–20, *19*
  Jebel al-Qal'a 14, 15
  Jordan Museum 19–20
  nymphaeum *19*
  Roman forum and theatre 18
  Temple of Hercules 15, *16*, 17
  Ummayad Palace 17–18
Ammonites 8, 14, 101, 208
Aqaba 194–6, *195*

Arabs 8, 15, 28, 37–9, 42, 63, 163, 169
  see also individual peoples
Aseikhin 78, 80, 81–2, *81*
Assyrians 14
Auranitis 70
Ayla 194
Ayyubids 79–80, 98, 120, 136, 155, 159
Azraq 78–80, *79*

B

Balu' 20
Baptism site of Christ 40
Baybars, Sultan 37, 136, 137, 155
Beihda 181–2
Bell, Gertrude 9, 11, 95, 98, 100, 166
Betthorus 123–5
Birkat ad-Darb 183
Birketein 34
Bosra 30, 63, 78, 163
Bozrah 147
Bronze Age 14, 21, 42, 45, 120, 210
Burckhardt, J.L. 10, 163, 183
Busayra 147–8, *149*
Byzantines 8, 31, 41, 42, 47, 52, 56, 67, 71, 76, 77, 105, 144, 155, 186, 197, 208, 210

C

Canaanites 42, 53
Cava de Suet 52